Crumbs from the Table

Articles in La Baguette
St Brelade's Parish Magazine
Summer 2011-Easter 2014

By Tony Bellows

ISBN: 978-1-326-40223-5

Contents

3

Introduction

In June 2011, I was contacted by Jeff Hathaway, the Editor of the St Brelade Parish Magazine, La Baguette, to submit a short article. He had been reading my blog – Tony's Musings - and somehow gained the impression that I could write. This was about limpets.

September 2011, and I submitted my second article about life saver Constance Brown. Then came a bombshell! Jeff was standing as a Deputy for St Brelade No 1, and wanted to ensure the magazine was seen to be strictly impartial and above the political arena. So he would be stepping down as editor for that edition, if I would like to be Honorary Guest Editor, to which I agreed. I still remember him showing me the mostly blank layout on his Quark program, and telling me – you are the editor – how are you going to fill it?!

What happened was that there were certain contributors – such as the WI – who could be relied on as regular contributors, and between us we thrashed out and brainstormed possible stories and interviews. I found – enjoyably – writing more than the one original article.

The collaboration worked well, and Jeff asked me to be Deputy Honorary Editor, and the pattern of collaboration also works well. We meet about a month and a half before an edition, and come up with possible stories and interviews. I have my list, he comes up with his, and we divide up who does what. In the meantime, there may be pending stories which have come up before our meeting, or ones which break afterwards.

The aim is a mixture of news stories and more general features, to give the magazine a nice degree of diversity, a kind of local reader's digest. Here are a number of articles I have penned since that fateful day in June 2011, and I hope you find them interesting and enjoyable.

Tony Bellows
September 2015

Limpet Gathering

And the story of a Connétable who became unstuck too!

THERE are many things that ordinary people do, that don't make it into the history books. Here is one personal anecdote.

In St Brelade's Bay, as a young boy, I would gather limpets with my sister from the rocks at the end of the bay. The trick is to take a small trowel, and rapidly slice into the rock below the base of the limpet, then it falls off complete. You have to be quick, or it suddenly grips hard, and is impossible to shift. Ours would be cooked for our cat, Spitfire, but during the Occupation, some Islanders had permission to forage for limpets to supplement their meagre diet. It is estimated that on diet of limpets alone, 400 would be needed daily for enough calories, so they would have been hard pressed to find enough to eat!

The Latin name for a limpet is *patella vulgata*, which is a description of what it looks like - it means "common kneecap", and if you look at a limpet, it does indeed look something like a kneecap, especially if you had knobbly knees, like I did as a young boy.

Limpets can also be found on the granite walls of St Brelade's Church. Look at the walls by the windows just as you enter, and there they are, the empty shells of limpets from ages past. What tales they could tell!

One story that the limpets might tell dates from 1708. Before the present Parish Hall was located at St Aubin, and before the Church Hall was built, Parish Assemblies were held within the Church itself.

During one Assembly, the Constable lost his temper, and swore. That was not done in a Church! So one Sunday a shocked congregation heard the Rector, standing in the pulpit, excommunicating the Constable, Monsieur Pipon, "cut off from the Body of Christ as a septic limb". He could no longer attend Parish Assemblies until he had shown public contrition in front of the congregation, because no excommunicated person could enter a church.

I wonder if any Rectors in modern times have felt regret at losing that power over their Constables!

Summer Edition 2011

Spirit of Christmas

Now's the time for making Sloe Gin

AUTUMN is upon us, in Keat's words, the "season of mists and mellow fruitfulness".

Blackberries, of course, are ripening to be picked, but another pastime for the season is the picking of sloes to make sloe gin. The sloe is the fruit of the blackthorn bush and it ripens in autumn, during September in Jersey, but later in England.

Sloes vary in size from a small olive to a large grape, but round, black and firm, with a large stone in relation to pulp.

If they are still slightly green or rock hard then they are not quite ripe, the flesh should give slightly but not soft like a plum even though they are from the same family.

You normally find that if it's a good season for plums then the same will ring true for sloes.

Take a litre bottle of gin and decant half into an empty bottle. Either prick sloes all over or make several little cuts in them (it doesn't seem to matter which you do as both ways give the same results - and it is actually quicker to cut rather than laboriously make 20 or more pricks in each sloe).

Add sloes until nearly all the gin (the half left in the bottle) is displaced and add about 6 8oz sugar. Put on the lid and turn a few times each day for a week until the sugar has dissolved, then every week for the next month, then whenever you think about it.

Sloe gin is best kept a minimum of 6 months before decanting but there is nothing to stop you drinking it after a couple of months. However, it does improve with age and most people make this years for consumption the following year.

Autumn Edition 2011

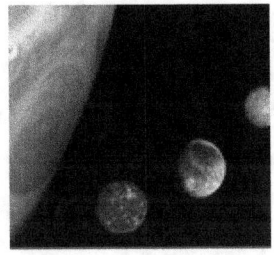

Stars in their eyes

An astronomical gathering visits St. Brelade

The British Astronomical Association (BAA) held their annual meeting, the largest gathering of professional and amateur British astronomers, at the Radisson Hotel in September.

BAA members were invited to a Jersey Astronomy Club Open Night at their headquarters, the Sir Patrick Moore observatory at Les Creux Country Park. About 40 people attended to look through the telescope at the night sky. Two members of the Guernsey Astronomy Society also attended.

Despite the patchy cloud cover, the skies cleared enough see most of the night sky. Comet Garradd was particularly notable that evening and could be seen through binoculars. Jupiter also dominates the night sky, rising well before 10pm at the start of the month, rising higher in the sky before dawn in the constellation of Aries. Its four biggest moons, Io, Europa, Callisto and Ganymede could be seen through binoculars.

The Jersey Astronomy Club are keen to get budding star gazers involved and all those interested in astronomy are welcome at their meetings. Owning a telescope is not a requirement. The Club holds its monthly meetings on the second Monday of every month (except in August) at 8.00pm on. Children cannot be left unattended and must be accompanied at all times by an adult.

Autumn Edition 2011

Winter Visitors

The geese who choose St. Brelade as their holiday destination

ST. AUBIN'S Harbour is where you might often see geese, but what may not be realised is that there are two different species who live there. One local and permanently resident, and the other seasonal, choosing Jersey as their winter holiday destination.

Jersey is already well known for being host to Dark-bellied Brent geese who travel from their nesting sites above the Arctic Circle and the plains of Siberia making an 8,000 mile journey. They start arriving in Jersey generally during October and November and by January their numbers are often in excess of 1,000 individuals. "The first record of them in a Jersey history book was way back in 1694" says local conservationist and bird expert Mike Stentiford. "They are attracted to the sea grasses growing off the island's coast. But they don't stay at St Aubin's harbour. The harbour area is instead temporary home to Pale-bellied Brent geese during the winter, and although they look similar, they actually fly in from Canada."

Mike Stentiford says: "This is what makes them so special as there are only a half-dozen other areas (in France and Ireland) where these Canadian immigrants winter. Because of the muddy waters around the periphery of St Aubin's harbour, a perfect food source can be found such as eel-grass, seaweed and mussels."

But what about the geese seen during our summer months at St Aubin's harbour? The ones whom Mike says "have a bit of an 'avian club' whereby life is all about loitering with little intent!"

These are Greylag geese, who at some time in the past escaped or were let loose by their owner. They can be easily distinguished from Brents by their orange bills. Local birdwatcher Bertram Bree says stray Greylag geese are also quite commonly found on the French mainland close to us. Once domesticated, many have now become wild. The Greylag Geese, however, have their own importance. Bertram notes that it was this species of geese which formed the basis of famous zoologist Konrad Lorenz's work on 'imprinting'; this is where younger geese 'imprint on their parents' as goslings, latching after them and following them around to learn their habits.

In St Aubin's Harbour, they sometimes seem to 'imprint' on the people, when they wander up the slipway and into the road after them, looking for hand-outs.

Pale-bellied Brent geese are the smallest of the goose family and color rings have used to plot their departure from Canada and arrival in St Aubin. They are darker than the Greylags, and have distinct white bellies, and usually around 40 of them, arrive in September. But they can also be distinguished by their feeding habits. Mike comments: "Whereas Brents are specialised feeders, the feral Greylags have a fairly open mind on what they eat - scraps from the public and anything they can find on the seashore."

Autumn Edition 2011

Whitley Bay to St Brelades Bay

"You have to take the opportunities if they crop up"

Number nine in a series of profiles featuring one of our regular advertisers, and those behind the businesses in acknowledgement of their invaluable support and generosity upon which the publication of this newsletter depends. In this edition, La Baguette Guest Editor, Tony Bellows talks to Paul Gambling, of the Sugareef Bar and Grill, St. Brelades Bay

PAUL GAMBLING, the owner of the Sugareef Bar & Grill in St. Brelade's Bay, is an authentic Geordie. He came from a very close family, with two brothers and a sister, and was born in the year that Newcastle United nearly won the Football League Cup Final. Perhaps because of that, he's been a lifelong supporter of the Magpies since childhood.

Newcastle is a large town, but Paul spent much of his childhood in nearby Whitley Bay. "I love the beach life," he said, and has happy recollections of the permanent seaside fairground '

The Spanish City', which at the time was owned by a fellow Geordie and entrepreneur living in Jersey, who would later give Paul a life changing opportunity.

A hard worker, as a teenager, Paul had a number of part time jobs, starting at 2 am, and finishing at 8 am - and then go on to do a full day's schooling at the George Stephenson High School. He also soon became a regular for stints as a DJ in the evenings. He was, he says, "pretty independent at a young age."

As the name might suggest, the George Stephenson High School, named after the famous inventor, had a bias towards engineering. Alongside electronics and science, Paul also did a course on Motor Vehicle Technology in which the class members took clapped out old vehicles, and repaired them to pass an MOT.

Leaving school at 18, he took a job at a large hotel chain where he learned the trade by taking on a number of jobs within the hotel, training to be a hotel manager, and enjoying the catering side especially. He was about to start a management training course, when the opportunity arose for a summer season as a DJ in Jersey, working for an entertainment complex owned by the former 'Spanish City' owner. He accepted, little realising that he would be taking up a more permanent residence in the Island. He says "you have to take the opportunities if they come up."

He was a resident DJ at Rock Galaxy in the late 1990s, later moving to Liquid Nightclub, then on to La Cala Restaurant and Nightclub in a managerial roll. He found his hotel background useful, as for events such as dinner dances, he would be co-ordinating caterers and musicians and marketing.

At the same time, he still spent time as a DJ elsewhere in places such as London, where his versatility and range with different kinds of music made him popular. "It's not just about playing records," he said, "you also have to understand body language, and see how the audience is responding to the music, and tailor it accordingly". His reputation led to spots alongside stars such as Eric Clapton.

About two and a half years ago, the opportunity came to take over what was then Tam's Safari Bars in St Brelade's Bay. Tam's had a "a bit of a reputation as a drinking hole", he said, "and I had to show that renaming the place 'SugaReef' was not just a cosmetic change of name, but a change in the whole ethos, to a relaxed and family friendly bar & restaurant serving great food". It's been a bigchallenge to turn it around, but now people are realising that it is a good place serving nice food - one with wonderful sea views. "I'd sooner be working in St Brelade's Bay, where I can just look out and see the sea, you never get tired of this view no matter what the weather", he said.

He enjoys walking his dogs on the beach in the winter, with his wife, and when he can find the time, likes to swim and water ski. For holidays, he likes to go abroad and ski in Europe. "I always try to find somewhere slightly different. We went to Transylvania earlier this year to ski which was great", he says.

For the moment, he is enjoying life to the full at Sugareef, but he has the notion that "one day it would be nice to run a beachside cafe in Miami." But he is proud of what he has achieved so far, in the journey, as he says has taken him, "from Whitley Bay to St Brelade's Bay".

Autumn Edition 2011

The Life Saver

The story of Constance Brown MBE

THERE can be treacherous currents in St Brelade's Bay which can sweep in and catch the unwary. Today we have trusty RNLI lifeguards keeping a sharp eye out for swimmers in trouble. Before the days of paid lifeguards, one resident of St Brelade's Bay saved many lives. This is her story.

Born in Blackburn, Lancashire, in 1904, Constance Brown came to Jersey in 1919 with her parents. After her father died in 1929, she and her mother built and ran Brown's CafÃ© in St Brelade's Bay, on the site of the recently closed Zanzibar restaurant. After 1945, she moved to 'Mimosa', a small bungalow next door.

Her first sea rescue was in August 1926 and her last in August 1958. Between those years she rescued or helped to rescue at least 30 people in St Brelade's Bay. She was a founder member of the Jersey Lifeguard Club set up in 1953, and also received the bronze medallion of the Royal Life Saving Society and a qualifying certificate of the Surf Lifesaving Association of Australia. In 1967, in recognition of her voluntary lifesaving work over 40 years she received an MBE.

It was over the years at her cafe, looking out into the bay, that she grew to recognise a dangerous sea on the incoming spring tides, as the current swept around the rocks on the Ouaisne side of St Brelade.

"I can smell and hear a wicked sea, I have been down and warned people on the beach not to bathe. The currents are always changing and the strong pull takes people onto the rocks or out to sea" she said in an interview in 1967.

Sometimes she entered the water fully clothed, and she was also injured during one rescue when her back was ripped on rocks as she was pulled by a lifeline. On three consecutive afternoons in one summer she personally rescued a total of four people and on another occasion, she rescued four at one time.

But she was also active in campaigning for the placing of lifesaving equipment on Jersey's beaches, for the organisation of voluntary beach patrols and, eventually, the establishment of a professional beach guard service, and this legacy endures today, making the beach safer for swimmers. "We proved the need for the paid lifeguards and they do a very good job in the bay" she said.

Autumn Edition 2011

Oldest immigrants

Excavations at La Cotte this year reveal more about Jersey's earliest inhabitants

THE cave at La Cotte de St Brelade, at the end of Quaisne Bay, and just below Portelet Common, has long been known to be the site of the earliest habitation in Jersey. Neanderthal man lived here around 250,000 years ago - the earliest record we have of the occupation of the Channel Islands by an intelligent species. The Neanderthals are named after their discovery in the Neander Valley, close to DÃ¼sseldorf in Germany. They died out only around 30,000 years ago, and were close enough cousins to human beings to interbreed. They were like us, only shorter, more heavily built and much stronger, particularly in the arms and hands, and with a thick bony brow ridge. No one knows for certain the reason why they died out.

The cave at La Cotte was inhabited by these hunter-gatherer tribes in between Ice Ages, spanning a period of over a quarter of a million years, adapting to the climate changes. They lived in a bleak land on the edge of the snows and glaciers that were even then receding northward.

Evidence suggests they hunted in groups, stampeding woolly mammoths with short spears to drive them across the granite headland and over the cliff. Then they would light fires, cook the meat and feast.

A new look at the cave this year has revealed more about our earliest immigrants. "Archaeologists have developed new ways of looking at stone tools since La Cotte de St Brelade was excavated in the 1970s," says Dr Beccy Scott from the British Museum and the Ancient Human Occupation of Britain project who is investigating the site. "Neanderthals were travelling to Jersey already equipped with good quality flint tools, then reworking them, very, very carefully so as not to waste anything. They were extremely good at recycling."

Flint is not a native rock to Jersey, so the Neanderthals had to bring it with them; it was a versatile rock, suitable for shaping stone arrow heads, spear heads and knives.

A cave in granite is unusual, and it is not surprising that there have been dangerous rock falls there. For public safety, the cave is barricaded off with barbed wire and a locked gate, and only accessible by archaeologists working under controlled conditions.

Autumn Edition 2011

Rock is not so solid

As a 'granite Parish', is St. Brelade at risk from radon?

THERE'S a surprising amount of uranium in granite, and this decays to radium, and that breaks down and produces radon gas. The gas moves slowly through tiny cracks in the rock strata and out into the air. Outside, it just gets blown away, but the danger lies when it seeps into contained areas and cannot easily escape, and then it is possible for concentrations to build up to levels that may pose a threat to health, often in the foundations and basements of houses.

Radon does have risks, and it is responsible for around for about 2,500 lung cancer deaths a year in the United Kingdom (about 5% of the total). The risk is greater if an individual smokes and is exposed to high levels of radon. But the risk to the average Parishioner is relatively small; statistically you are probably far more likely to be run over by a car while crossing the road at Red Houses!

Jersey's had several surveys for radon gas, and there might be another one soon, as the public become more aware of the risk. Surveys are simple to undertake. They merely involve the installation of a small passive detector in a house for three months.

And there is no need to panic, because if your house did have higher levels of radon than are judged safe, installing ventilation equipment or making sure the house is properly ventilated will make the home safe again.

So when colder weather comes, and annoying draughts sweep under doors, it is comforting to realise that they are blowing away the risks too.

Autumn Edition 2011

Granville/Jersey swim Veterans group crawl home

NORMALLY when people from St Brelade visit their French twin town of Granville, and the neighbouring villages in Normandy, they sail there and back either via the Gorey ferry or from the Albert Quai in St. Helier or by a private boat.

Not always so it seems. St. Brelade residents, Neil Faudemer and Sue Coombs completed the crossing from Anneville-sur-Mer, near Granville back to Jersey by swimming! Neil and Sue were part of a relay team of six veteran swimmers who swam the 20 nautical miles, while avoiding large swarms of jellyfish and strong tidal flows, to get back to the Island. Other members of the team included Dave Le Clercq, Steve Toudic, Stuart Banks and Ken Huish.

The team left France at 8.30 am on Saturday, each taking a turn to take the plunge from their boat and swim several legs of the journey back. The team challenge ended at 6.42 pm when Mrs Coombes (pictured opposite with Ken Huish) arrived back in Jersey, coming ashore at Anne Port Bay in St. Martin on Jersey's east coast.

Neil said: "I think I might take the ferry next time, not that I didn't enjoy the swim, but my duty frees got rather wet!"

Autumn Edition 2011

Heavens above, its Venus!

Jersey Astronomy Club invite you to watch the 'Evening Star'

THE Astronomy Club met on 14th November, and listened to a short talk by Martin Ahier on the moons of Jupiter. This was followed by a talk by Tony Isherwood on the use of different coloured filters to enhance the viewing of planets with telescopes, and he passed a filter wheel around for everyone to look through.

Although there was some haze, the night was clear enough for members to go out to the observatory, where Jupiter could be seen through the telescope; its two dark bands in the northern hemisphere and southern hemisphere being clearly visible through the lens.

In December, Venus will be the planet to watch out for. The "Evening Star" is visible low in the south-western sky immediately after sunset, and is so intensely bright that it can be seen with the naked eye even while the sky is still light. At the start of December, Venus sets just after 5 pm, but by the end of the month it can seen until after 6.30 pm, when the sky is quite dark. At that time, it is quite unmistakable, as the brightest star-like object in the sky.

Christmas Edition 2011

Bouonne santé!

A 'tongue-in-cheek' story to mull over this Christmas
by Stan A Claus

CHRISTMAS is a time for tall tales told around the fireside, sipping mulled wine, and eating mince pies, and here is a slightly different version of the Santa story told by Mr Claus (of La Moye).

"I was born in the village of Patara, Turkey, and came from a very poor family. I still remember when our fortunes changed for the better, when I looked out to sea, and I saw three ships come sailing by. One of the people on a ship was a trader who came to our village, and he challenged us to a game of cards, asking us whether we wanted to 'deal or no deal". I still remember his Christian name, because he was the first Noel that I came across.

As a young boy, I always enjoyed singing in the choir, and taking part in processions; sometimes I would get to play the part of a little drummer boy. With my religious background, it was not surprising that I became a Bishop. The people were quite poor, so I used to go around the city and countryside, on a silent night, just before Christmas, putting presents in children's socks. Not many people were up at that hour, but I remember seeing shepherds watching their flocks by night, although the younger animals would be kept inside, away in a manger.

As I passed the Royal Palace, I would see a curtain twitch, as Good King Wenceslas looked out. He was one of three kings living close by, who had originally come from the Orient.

As a Bishop, I set off on my travels, and came to Holland, where I learnt that my name was Sinter Klaus in Dutch, which sounded rather sinister, so I emigrated to America, and changed my name to Santa Claus.

But after a spell in America, I decided to set up a charity at the North Pole, and moved there. I had married a very nice lady called Adeste Fideles, and we had two daughters, called Holly and Ivy. They didn't really want any presents themselves, although I do remember when they were five, they told me that all they wanted for Christmas was their two front teeth. Later, in their teens, they used to be Rockin' Around the Christmas Tree.

People often ask what I do the rest of the year. Well, in January I take a well earned break in the Isle of Wight. I hope that the weather will let it snow, and dream of a Wight Christmas, when I can rest, a merry gentleman.

To the readers of La Baguette, I have this seasonal message "A very Merry Christmas Everybody".

Christmas Edition 2011

Christmas Pud Adventure

Stirring up the history of one of the most essential festive treats

NOWADAYS, most Christmas puddings are bought from shops, but the day they traditionally started being made was called "Stir-Up Sunday". This fell on 20 November 2011 this year, and is the last Sunday in the Christian calendar before Advent, the period of preparation in the run up to Christmas.

The opening words for the 'collect' or prayer to start that Sunday in the Book of Common Prayer were "Stir up, we beseech thee, O Lord, the wills of thy faithful people; that they, plenteously bringing forth the fruit of good works...", and from that, the Sunday took its name.

It was an easy reminder for cooks to get out their ingredients and start making and stirring up the Christmas pudding, since the pudding mixture needs to stand for several weeks before cooking.

The pudding mixture was always stirred from east to west - which meant clockwise - in honour of the three Wise men who came from the East to visit the infant Jesus, and each member of the family in turn, would take part in stirring the mixture, and making a wish while they did so. It was also said that the longer you stirred, the more good luck you would have in the coming year, which was probably a cunning ruse by a sly Victorian cook!

Various small items were traditionally also added to the mix such as a sixpence (which was a small silver coloured pre-decimal coin), a button, a thimble, and a ring.

If you found a sixpence, it was expected that you would die rich. A button meant you would have new clothes next year. A thimble indicated that you would never marry and remain a bachelor or old maid. But a ring meant that you would be married within the year!

The dangers of swallowing such items and damaging teeth on them means that this custom has not been adopted by the commercial Christmas pudding manufacturers.

Agatha Christie was very fond of Christmas, and her fictional detective Hercule Poirot attended a celebration of Christmas in a country house, where in addition to the various small items, a thief had attempted to hide a Royal ruby in a Christmas pudding.

As well as the jewel, which Poirot recovers, it pictures all the things we associate with Christmas - an old country house, a decorated Christmas tree, turkey, a blazing log fire, and a walk across the snowy fields to the Church for Midnight Mass.

Enjoy your Christmas pudding, but don't expect any Royal rubies in it!

Christmas Edition 2011

'Twas the night before Christmas'

A festive poem for St. Breladiase

'Twas the night before Christmas, and all through St Brelade
Not a creature was stirring, from house to boatyard
The double decker had gone, the final bus fare
Long gone were shoppers from Quennevais Square

The children were nestled all snug in their beds,
And the allotments were quiet, no light in their sheds
Now St Aubin's was sleeping, with no geese in a flap
And beach shops had closed for a long winter's nap.

When in Reg's Garden, there arose such a clatter
He sprang from the bed to see what was the matter.
Glimpsed a red sleigh there, which went in a flash
Not speeding past 30, but still making a dash

Santa was coming, from La Haule to Corbiere
And his red sleigh sped by, with the tiny reindeer
Bouan Noue, he cried, as it passed every house
Where no creature was stirring, not even a mouse

And in the morning, while church bells rang out
The children exclaimed, with glee and a shout
As they saw presents, by the Christmas tree light
And the stockings of toys, that came in the night.

Back under attack!

Olliviers Farm residents .. it may not be end of the matter

IN October recently appointed Planning and Environment Minister Deputy Rob Duhamel, decided to reject the application to build eight cottages on the Olliviers Farm caravan site, ending a year of uncertainty and worry for the residents there. There had been 526 objections to the plans.

Ollivier's Farm is a site unique to Jersey, an informal settlement of 19 caravans and chalets at Ouaisne. But as resident Mark Winter says, 'a lot of people didn't even know it's here'

It dates back to the 1930s, and the oldest resident, 82-year-old John Wakeham (pictured opposite) has lived there for more than half a century. He remembers when the Island Beauty Committee (now part of Planning and Environment), instituted a policy that forbade caravans to be brought into the Island. Existing caravans were permitted, but when his was damaged in a fire, he was told he could not replace it, only rebuild it, which he did.

The site is well maintained, but residents have been holding off all but essential maintenance over the last year, because they had been in a state of limbo, waiting for a decision from the Planning Department. It blends well into its surroundings, and John Wakeham said that 'there had been enough building and spoiling the coastline.'

The nearby Ouaisne Common is a site of special interest, one of Jersey's richest and most diverse nature reserves, and is probably best known as the habitat of the agile frog. The residents are very aware of this, and help to care for the locality, being sensitive to their living on the hinterland of this special environment.

Another resident who had been living there since 1996 said that it was "a great community, where we all help each other and stick together".

However since Mr Winter's comments to La Baguette it has been announced that the decision is to be appealed by the owner, once again causing anxiety amongst the residents.

Christmas Edition 2011

Christmas drop-in

The Constable and Deputies plan Christmas open house at Communicare

FROM 3pm - 6pm on Friday 16th December, in the Cargill Room at Communicare, there is an opportunity for Parishioners to drop-in and meet the Constable Steve Pallett and Parish Deputies, Sean Power, Montfort Tadier and John Young, and for our States Members to wish their Parishioners a very merry Christmas, over a cup of tea and a mince pie - or two.

The Christmas "Drop in Afternoon Tea", is open to everyone in the Parish who would like to meet with our newly elected and re-elected States representatives, either just for light conversation, or to raise any issues they may have, rather more informally.

Tea, coffee, cakes and mince pies will be available, and La Baguette has been told that some form of musical entertainment has also been promised!

Christmas Edition 2011

The Western Railway

Memories of Don Filleul, a former States member, and St Brelade Parishioner.

DON was born at Greve d'Azette in 1926, very close to the station of the Jersey Eastern Railway. He still has very early memories of those trains. "I can remember travelling to Gorey, and to the Snow Hill terminus.", he says, "And thus began a lifetime devotion to railways."

The Jersey Eastern Railway ceased to run on 21 June 1929, because of declining profits, and henceforth, train excursions were on the Western Railway. The young master Filleul was taken frequently to Corbiere on the Western Railway, mostly with an aunt as his main companion on these journeys. Some of the coaches can still be seen at Pallot's Steam Museum, with their facing seats, and no corridors between carriages.

There was little to offer at Corbiere but the view, so they just returned, but for the young boy, travelling by train was enjoyable in itself. "It must have taken about half an hour from Town to St. Aubin", he recalls, "and there was a wait there before the onward journey to Corbiere."

He remembers that he developed preferences for certain engines, and also disliked others - "Anyone remember the one painted light green? I didn't care for that." He was intensely interested in the engines, all of which had names. But he never got to speak to the drivers - "Auntie did not allow me to make friends with the drivers. In those days such contact was out of order."

By the 1930s, the Jersey Railway was under pressure from the buses which could travel over a wider catchment area than trains.

During the winter, all the rolling stock of the Jersey Railway was stored in the St Aubin station, and on the night of 16 October 1936, a fire broke out. This destroyed much of the station building, 15 of the carriages, and damaged the Terminus Hotel. Don's father took him to see the devastation. "The horror of course was the fire at St. Aubin's station, the destroyed coaches the awful stench of the place is almost still with me.", he recalls, "Dad took me there - he was also a bit soft about trains, and we stared with sadness at the catastrophe."

That was the final blow to the already struggling railway company, and it was decided to close the railway entirely. The track and remaining rolling stock was sold off, and the way between St Aubin and Corbiere became a public walk, which it remains to this day.

The Terminus Hotel later became the Parish Hall and offices, replacing the use of the Church Hall at St Brelade's Church for Parish Assemblies.

Christmas Edition 2011

Frightfully good combo!

Lavender Farm is new haunt for Halloween half term family fun

The Lavender Farm was the venue for family fun, when they held a "Halloween Half Term" from the 25th to the 30th October. With Bingo style cards to complete, young children and parents explored the "Spooky Haunted Gardens" looking for clues in the Monster Hunt.

Every child who dressed up was also given a free cupcake, and extra treats were also given by the "Witch in Residence", who hovered around the grounds every afternoon; children who found and collected feathers for her cauldron were given sweets.

La Baguette's reporter spoke to Izzy, the Witch in residence, by the side of the old Gypsy Caravan. "A lot of the kids have dressed up, and there have been some really good costumes," she said, "I've seen witches, grim reapers, skeletons, ghosts and vampires wandering around looking for clues".

Inside the cafe, there was a pumpkin design competition, where children could draw a pumpkin on paper, and a winning design would be pulled out of the witch's hat, and the face carved out on a real pumpkin, for the winner to take home for Halloween Monday.

The idea of having a week's fun at the Lavender Farm over half term was the idea of Kate Whatuira, the chef at the Lavender Farm. As she carved out a pumpkin, she said that they had been extremely fortunate to have good weather, and this brought the season to a successful close.

Art of beachcombing

World Beach Art Championships held on Parish beaches

ON the 29th October, the World Beach Art Championships organised by Jersey Tourism began on Ouaisne beach. Artists included local sand worker Andy Coutanche, and international stars including Andres Amador from California, Andy Moss from the United Kingdom and Sam Dougados from France.

But it was also a day for all the family to participate, and take a rake and enjoy drawing pictures in the sand themselves. Hundreds of Islanders came to the bay, and the St Brelade Honorary Police were helpfully on hand to divert traffic when the car park at Ouaisne was full up.

Food was available too, where Marcus Calvani from La Cantina and his team showed how to dig a fire pit and use hot stones and seaweed for the method of cooking known as a "clam bake", where local produce, such as lobster, was steamed until ready to eat. The food was all available to purchase and consume by Islanders, raising money for Channel Islands Air Search. There was plenty to eat, with other local restaurants and pubs also providing food, including a tasty hog roast bun with apple sauce, cooked and carved during the afternoon. There were also guided walks every hour, which included local history talks about nearby La Cotte Cave, which were hosted by the Societe Jerriais, Jersey Heritage and Environmental Services.

On the Sunday the Grand Finale saw the international beach art champions set off to other designated Island beaches, including St Brelades Bay, to ply their skills, with four hours to prepare their masterpiece. The award ceremony took place at the Beach House in Ouaisne, and the winning artist was Frenchman Sam Dougados, with a geometric design. He was awarded a prize and crowned champion of the MyMemory.com Beach Art World Championships Jersey 2011.

Mr Dougados said: "This award is a great honour and very much unexpected. I feel that everyone was a winner today as each piece of art was a masterpiece in its own right. It was a privilege to be invited and I very much look forward to next year's event."

Christmas Edition 2011

New Procureur

Arthur Morley elected Procureur following retirement of Reg Langlois.

FOLLOWING the retirement of Reg Langlois, Arthur Morley (66) and one of the Parish Centeniers, was elected as Parish Procureur on Tuesday 14th February.

Arthur was proposed by Senator Sarah Ferguson and his nomination paper was signed by no less that 3 former Constables- all of whom he served under during his 15 years of Honorary Service. Arthur brings to the role a wealth of experience not only of the Parish, but the professional skills from his background in the finance industry being a former senior manager with the Jersey Financial Services Commission.

Arthur succeeds Reg Langlois who had been one of two Procureur's for the last three years.

Reg told La Baguette: "The role can be demanding at times, but I am proud to have been able to serve the Parish and during my six years been able to see through many projects including the Maison St. Brelade new-build and refurbishment."

In congratulating Arthur on his election Constable Steve Pallett said that he was looking forward to working with the Procureurs and that the Parish had a strong and capable team.

Easter Edition 2012

Planning Group

All new development to be scrutinised by the Parish', says Constable

IN a letter to the media outlining his concerns, Constable Steve Pallet advised of his approval of the setting up of an independent 'Planning Group' to monitor new large scale developments proposed in the Parish. In his letter Constable Pallet said:

"I have for sometime been concerned with the issue of over-development and inappropriate design that I believe has damaged the natural beauty of parts of St. Brelade. The recently completed development at Portelet and the widely criticised Station House scheme at Corbiere not only highlight my personal concerns but that of parishioners who are increasingly of the opinion that further ill-considered development of our coastline must be avoided at all costs."

"Protection of our coastal areas against poor development, especially those that border the designated National Park and Green Zone, have become a priority. The Parish Deputies also share my view. 'Garden grabbing' is another area of development that in recent years has crept to a point where our Parish characteristics and environment are being severely damaged. "

"To stem what appears to be a tide of inappropriate development in St. Brelade and to protect the unique and acknowledged beauty of its rural areas and natural coastline it has now become important that we take measures to ensure that all new development is also scrutinised by the Parish. It is crucial that parishioners are kept fully advised of schemes, that while directly affecting specific residents, often have much wider implications for the local community, if not the Island as a whole."

"My particular concern is that architects place copyright upon their drawings thus preventing the media from fully reporting upon the full visual impact of their schemes. Commercial copyright is one thing, but since plans are already available to the public on application, I see no reason why any developer would want to restrict opportunity for the media to publish them unless they disagree with the need for total openness. "

"As Constable and States member I have great sympathy for the Planning Applications Panel who not only have to deal with the practical and emotive side of contentious applications that are often caused by simple lack of transparency and communication, but also to consider the complicated States planning policies applying to individual applications."

During the recent elections the setting up of a Watchdog Group in St. Brelade to monitor planning applications in the Parish was suggested by one of the candidates. This was later echoed in broader terms by the Planning Minister, Rob Duhamel, who at a Parish meeting to discuss issues affecting St. Aubin, also indicated his support of the idea."☐ That group is now in the process of being formed and hopes to become fully active in late spring.

Constable Pallett told La Baguette: "I am happy to support the group. It is not specifically designed to oppose schemes, nor is it anti-development, but rather to act as a consultation conduit between developers parishioners and the Parish whereby proposals can be openly discussed, and objections fully explored."

Easter Edition 2012

41

Star attraction

St. Brelades beach is a hit!

In 2011, St Brelade's beach was voted the sixth most beautiful beach in Britain, but this year, it has been voted the second most beautiful beach in Britain, only beaten by Bournemouth. The chart compiled by the world's largest travel website, Tripadvisor, is based on hotels, restaurants, parking and amenities as well as appearances.

An extra attraction this year, alongside the rock pools at the end of the bay, is the remains of a meteor which was seen shooting across British skies in early March. It was spotted over much of the UK heading south across Devon, and there was speculation that it would land in Normandy. But in fact it arrived in Jersey. April Masterman of the Jersey Astronomy Club saw it come down at the end of St. Brelade's Bay. She said it was "the most amazing thing I have seen in the night sky in ages - unbelievable".

It was positively identified as the meteor on 1st April when a group of enthusiasts went to investigate the object which they say consists largely of iron pyrites, a substance that is often to referred to as 'Fools Gold.'

[Easter April Fool 2012]
Easter Edition 2012

Bobby Jo on the beat

Working together with the Parish

A RECENT Police initiative in Jersey is geographical policing. Each shift has an area that they are responsible for. In the West of Jersey, the district is St Peter, St Ouen and St Brelade.

Overall oversight is provided by Inspector Harry Carre, and PC Jo Carter is the lead uniform officer allocated to this district. She has special training for family liaison, sexual offences liaison and public order matters, and is fluent in Portuguese and Spanish "" all qualifications ideal for working in a small community.

Her shift may be daytime, evening or night, and she drives out to patrol the district. She will check in at the Parish Hall for any incidents and reports to follow up, and meets the Chef de Police regularly.

She also attends the monthly meetings of the Honorary Police, and they may come out on patrol with her, working together as a team. The Honorary Police today have professional training, and she can use her 13+ years experience in the States of Jersey Police to give them confidence when handling difficult incidents. There is also good liaison with schools to help children with problems stay out of serious trouble, as part of a multi-agency team; she also gets to know children so they see her as someone approachable for help and assistance.

In daytime, she may also be out and about on foot patrol; in St Brelade's Parish, for example, this could be at Quennevais Precinct, Red Houses or down at St Aubin's Harbour, where she provides a friendly "bobby on the beat" police presence. She may also be present at public events with the Parishes.

Easter Edition 2012

Sticky problem

Protest over St. Aubin harbour silt

ON New Year's Day, Roy Deeming used his boat to block the entrance to the harbour as a "peaceful protest" to against the silting up of the harbour. Former Constable Mike Jackson told La Baguette that the silting up of St.Aubins harbour is a perennial problem:

"The design of the harbour is such that the problem has challenged successive Harbour masters since it was built in the 18th and 19th centuries. Opinions differ as to why silting occurs but it seems that a minute layer is added on each tide when it arrives in the harbour under suspension in the 'agitated' water then precipitates out as it settles down. Periods of heavy rain add alluvial deposits from the brook running down through the harbour in addition to the sandy bank which appears at the end of the South arm particularly after a South Westerly storm. It is interesting to note that in days when cargoes were brought into St. Aubin by sailing ship it was mandatory for the vessels to be loaded with this sand and stone as ballast for the return journeys in the event that they were 'light' or as was termed 'in ballast'."

"In recent times, the harbour has been dredged every 12 years. The next dredging will take place in September 2012, and will necessitate the removal of all boats, buoys and chains. Excavators will then be able to set about removing the mud without getting entangled in the myriad of chains and ropes which 'lurk' beneath. The end of the year will hopefully see most of the mud cleared."

Branching out

Allotments benefit from Mizvah Day

TWO sweet chestnut trees have been planted at the entrance of Jersey's Les Creux allotments as part of a day of Jewish-led social action. Mitzvah Day, which fell on 20th November 2011, is a special day in the Jewish calendar based on the Jewish values of "tikkun olam" (repairing the world), "tzedek" (righteousness) and "gemilut chassadim" (acts of loving kindness).

Jewish congregations take part in community projects to reduce hardship and poverty in the world, and to help the environment. It is a "hands on" day rather than a fund raising event.

Planting the trees were Stephen Regal and Martha Bernstein of Jersey's Jewish Congregation, with Conrad Evans of Jersey Trees for Life, Judith Davey from St Brelade's Church, Parish Les Creux Allotment Committee member Reg Langlois and Jeff Hathaway, Chairman of the Jersey Allotments and Leisure Gardening Association (JALGA).

Jeff Hathaway said:

"It's a wonderful gesture and so appropriate at this 'giving' time of year for both the Jewish and Christian communities. We are deeply grateful."

Sweet chestnuts are very versatile and well suited to Les Creux. Apart from producing an edible crop, they are able to withstand drought and poor soil conditions and are great for wildlife in the area - particularly red squirrels.

Occupation: Concert parties

A Parishioner remembers.
Don Filleul talking to Tony Bellows

In this edition, La Baguette features more memories of Don Filleul OBE [86], a former States member, and now a St Brelade Parishioner.

IN 1941, when he was 15, Parish resident Don Filleul's family moved to Beaumont. He recalls that before the Germans began constructing their anti-tank wall that "all there had been between our house and the sea were the remains of Beaumont Station platform and lovely great lumps of golden granite which were the means of protection from the waves."

He remembers the Germans building the concrete wall and the bunker which is now the Gunsite Cafe. "The garrison was housed in the wooden hut, still there, beside the Round Tower, at the top of which lolled a German soldier with his twin anti-aircraft machine-gun. I recall him ringing his alarm bell and shouting "Achtung Flugzeug" when a reconnaissance Spitfire flew over at about 30,000 feet."

How did people occupy themselves in the Occupation? Don made friends with residents of the district, and became involved with what was called the "Cecil Corbin Concert Party". Graeme Huelin, a former Deputy in St Brelade, also took part. He also met his wife, Hilary Boniface, who also took part. The ensemble sang and danced; dancing under the tutelage of Miss Le Caudey of Beaumont.

They produced a number of shows held at the Hamon Hall, which was on Mont Les Vaux near to St Aubin's School. The hall was used for Parish Assemblies, but also was available for private hire. It is now a private dwelling. The most memorable show was "Streamline" which was also taken to a lot of Parish Halls by horse and van. He remembers that "after the show, we were treated with refreshments which revealed the vast difference between farmers' rations and our own!"

Easter Edition 2012

Royal Gardens

Country Fete is planned at Reg's Garden to celebrate Queen's Jubilee
by Tony Bellows

REG'S Garden is to be the venue for a St. Brelade Country Fete to celebrate the Queens Jubilee this summer.

Garden owner Reg Langlois told La Baguette:

"There is a lot of work to do before finalising the exact detail, but we are also hoping that a small profit can be made out of entrances so we can also make a a donation to local charities. But what I can say is that we are planning entertainment and food all day. This could be the biggest event that we have ever had in the garden!"

The event, which is being supported by the Parish, will be held on Sunday 3rd June from 11am to 7.30pm

Easter Edition 2012

JAC and the Bean Crock

Astronomy Club hold crock and pub quiz with star prize!

CLOUDY skies in February didn't dampen the enthusiasm of the Jersey Astronomy Club. At their meeting at the Patrick Moore Astronomy Center, members enjoyed a 'Pub Quiz and Bean Crock Night' with bean crock (both meat and vegetarian styles) and bread, provided by Rosemary & Tony Isherwood, Olive Lawrence & Jodie Masterman. Regulars were joined by the Constable, Steve Pallett and his wife and a 'scratch team' from La Baguette.

After the meal, the 20 question quiz ranged from simple astronomy posers such as "What is the largest planet in our solar system?, to more difficult ones such as: "Oh be a fine girl, kiss me right now!. What do the first letters of the words represent" (It is a mnemonic for remembering different kinds of stars).

The prize, a Concise Guide to Astronomy, was awarded to youngster Tom who won the quiz with 18 points. The La Baguette team managed a creditable 16. The Constable won the consolation prize - with 1 point!

Easter Edition 2012

Nicki's colourful Exhibition

Raising awareness of Parkinson's Disease

FROM 9th February to 3rd March 2012, there was an exhibition of paintings by Nicki Baudains at The Harbour Gallery, St Aubin. Entitled "Retrospective of Progress", it was a solo exhibition to raise awareness of early onset Parkinson's disease, and also funding for local support.

The exhibition was officially opened by radio presenter Murray Norton.

Nicki was diagnosed with early onset Parkinson's disease around three years ago. She noticed that while doing face painting with students at school, her left arm would become immobile, and the same 'freezing up' happened to her left side when doing every day actions like walking up stairs. "I'd reach the top stair, and then my leg just wouldn't move", said Nicki.

Many people have the idea that Parkinson's disease is to do with involuntary shaking and tremors but just as common is involuntary rigidity where the sufferer freezes into immobility. There is a lack of dopamine in the brain, so that signals to move limbs do not work properly. Another misconception is about age. Eileen Smith, the Chairlady of the local Parkinson's disease society spoke at the official opening of the exhibition, and said that it could strike people of any age.

Medication could help to keep it on a plateau for around 20 years, but even the best drugs had some side effects. But some of these could be beneficial. In Nicki's case, after taking medication, "suddenly there were all these colours and ideas in my head, I just needed to get them onto canvas".

Knit and natter

Blankets Romania bound

MARKLAND Hall, Communicare every Wednesday morning is the venue for a group of knitters from the Friendship Group busily knitting and chatting for a very worthwhile cause. They knit squares that are put together to create blankets that are collected by Rosemary Coote MBE of the Friends of Ecco Homo Trust. The large blankets are given to needy elderly people and smaller cot-sized ones are given to babies in poor and needy families in Romania.

The Friendship Group have been doing this for 14 years and the knitters don't always just knit at meetings as any squares that they do at home are brought along and put together. Stripey blankets are done with odd small amounts of wool and someone who can crochet makes a good edging to the completed blankets.

They are making a plea for anyone who can donate wool to telephone reception at Communicare and leave a message. Volunteers can collect if it's a problem to drop it off there. Double-ply is mostly used but anything will be used and very much appreciated.

Easter Edition 2012

Lent Lunches

Plus traditional Conger Eel Soup recipe

LENT is traditionally a time for giving up, and giving to others. Part of the Parish fund raising for Christian Aid during Lent is by Lent Lunches, which take place at St Brelade's Parish Hall on Fridays between noon and 2.00 pm, and are provided by members of St Brelade's Churches, each Church acting in rotation on successive Fridays.

For a modest donation, there is simple and tasty fare to enjoy - freshly made soups, bread, crackers and cheese (donated by Waitrose), with tea or coffee. The final lunch, Good Friday on April 6, 2012, always has two soups, one of which is Conger Eel Soup, a popular Jersey dish, cooked by the chef at Maison St Brelade.

Here is a recipe from the Jersey Island Federation of the Womens Institute:

1.5 lbs of conger eel
3 pints of water
1 heart of cabbage, chopped
2 leeks
Parsley, thyme and the petals of a marigold. 1 quart of Jersey Milk
1 oz of Jersey Butter

Boil conger in the water for three hours, strain and keep liquid. Remove the fish from the bone and return to the pot with the vegetables and marigold and season to taste. Bring to then boil and then add milk and butter to serve.

Supper Church

'New format opportunity to share thoughts' say organisers

THE popular "Supper Church" is continuing from April to September this year, but with a slightly different format. Supper Church meets in the upstairs room at the Smuggler's Inn, Ouaisne, usually on the first Thursday of every month, with a two course meal, drink and coffee, together an informal friendly discussion on a Christian theme.

Jo Mulliner from St Brelade's Church, who organises it alongside Brian Clarke also from St, Brelade's Church, says that "We will have a short introduction talk, followed by an open ended discussion at our tables while we eat, to assist the discussion some quotations will be handed out, and then we will give everyone an opportunity to share their thoughts and bring these views together over coffee."

The first time is free and thereafter is Â£15 for those who can afford to pay and a contribution if possible from those who can't pay. Everyone is welcome. The Theme for the summer programme is "What do Christians believe?" and will start on Wednesday 4th April (7pm) with the question: " Who is Jesus?"

Easter Edition 2012

Retiring Procureur

Reg Langlois retires after twenty years of Parish service.

REG Langlois retired as Parish Procureur earlier this year after six years in the post. The position of Procureur du Bien Publique is an honorary one whose duties ""as G.R. Balleine says, are "that of a trustee, elected by the Parish Assembly, whose main duty is to pass deeds or contracts, to conduct parish law-suits, and to keep a watchful eye on the Constable's finance." It is an important position, if mostly unseen by Parishioners.

Reg told La Baguette that he was asked on several occasions to take on the position of Procureur by the late Brian le Boutillier, whom he had known for over 60 years, and had taught Reg at Sunday School. "Brian taught me the value of service to the Parish", he said, "and so when I was asked to be Procureur, I naturally said yes".

Other positions Reg has held in the parish, were on the Rating Committee, Roads Committee and he also headed a small committee for Parish in Bloom for eleven years with which he took the parish into the finals of Britain in Bloom on two occasions. A project he has been involved in recently, in which he played a significant part, saw the setting up of the allotments with thirty-six plots at Les Creux.

Having served the Parish in honorary capacities for over 20 years, Reg has now decided to step down. "At 76, I am starting to feel my age, and thought that a spot of garden leave was in order". However, that doesn't mean the end of Reg's involvement in Parish affairs, because he was the organiser in the Jubilee Fete held at his garden, and there will be Regstock 5 later in the year.

Summer Edition 2012

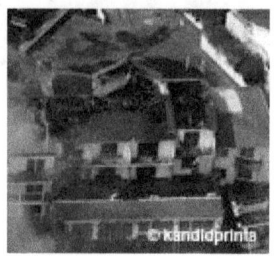

Minister renders opinion

Development approved with caveat

PLANNING Minister Rob Duhamel has approved plans to build nine plats on the site of the burnt out Mont de la Rocque Hotel, provided that the upper render is changed into a different colour to that lower down the building.

The proposals have met with fierce opposition from some St Aubin residents. The St Aubin Residents' Association called for a better scheme 'with true architectural merit'. Deputy John Young, St Brelade No.1 district which encompasses St. Aubin, said that the timescale had been rushed.

But Aaron Terry of Robert Limbrick Architects said changes had been made after listening to the planning applications panel, and the new design would 'get rid of the blot on the landscape that had been there since 2010.' With a photo of the burnt-out hotel, and one of the proposed new building, La Baguette's reporter went down to St. Aubin to gauge the reaction from passers by.

A passing jogger thought it looked fine, but wondered if the Island really needed another purpose build development 'to sell at extortionate rates'. A St Aubin resident suggested that it was 'the kind of building you can see in Spain', and wondered if that was really appropriate for St Aubin.

Visitors from London, on the other hand, thought that 'there was already a similar curved design lower down the hillside', so it would not be out of place, although they did wonder 'if the height might be out of place on the skyline'. And a couple from Essex thought the design wasn't bad - they had seen worse, but wondered if it might not be better faced with a local granite.

Summer Edition 2012

Sanctuary House drop-in

Sky-dive raises over £15,000 for charity

DONATIONS of £15,482 have been raised for Sanctuary House by St Brelade parishioner.and pensioner, Brian Clarke [70], who plans to jump out of an aeroplane from two miles above St Aubin's Bay. He will fall at around 130 miles and hour, completing a one mile drop in 30 seconds. The parachute will then open to complete the second mile depositing Brian safely on St Aubin's beach five minutes later.

Brian says "A little known fact about Jersey is that there is a high rate of suicide and in the past year, six men have committed suicide in the west of the Island and not far from St. Aubin. Sanctuary House in St Aubin is temporary accommodation for troubled, lonely and solitary men giving the support and help they need in order to get back into a more secure situation.

These men have made Sanctuary House into a family community and although many have 'graduated', they come back to help other men who are in the situation they used to be in" He runs a monthly group which meets for meals and discussion called 'Supper Church' and says that "about 20 of the men from Sanctuary House have been attending each month over the last year." He said: "I personally have got to know some of them and have seen personalities transformed over that time. I am convinced that this is a genuinely valuable project. It receives no financial support from the States of Jersey and relies entirely on volunteers and charitable gifts."

Parishioners Remember - Coronation Day 1953

BACK in 1953, there was a special airline day trip to go to London from Jersey offering Islanders the opportunity to see the Coronation procession of Queen Elizabeth II.

St Brelade Parishioner Ann Shepard saw this advertised at the specially reduced rate of £6 per person, in the JEP. That does not seem a great deal now, but her weekly take home pay back in 1953 was just £5, so it was more than one week's wages. But it was a chance of a lifetime, and she decided to go with her friend Beryl.

Along with other Islanders, the two 19 year olds had to be at the Weighbridge at 5.30 in the morning, where a coach took them to the Airport. The trip was popular, and she remembers that the Dakota airplane was full.

In the middle of the flight to England, the Captain announced over the communications system that news had just been received that Sir Edmund Hillary had reached the summit of Mount Everest. He was the first climber to achieve that goal.

The press called the successful ascent a coronation gift. In London, they took a train to Hyde Park, where they saw the Queen and the Coronation Procession proceeding along Birdcage Walk, followed by all the other dignitaries, most notably Salote, Queen of Tonga, in her open carriage. After the Coronation, they saw the Queen again, now processing towards Buckingham Palace.

After the crowds had gone, Ann and Beryl made friends with two young South African men, who had also been watching the show, and they were treated to a meal out. But all too soon, it was time to get the plane back to Jersey, and Ann remembers being so tired that she slept for the entire flight. But it had been a memorable day, and one she still treasures.

Summer Edition 2012

Did you Know?

Interesting Jubilee facts compiled by Tony Bellows

• THE word 'jubilee' means a loud, joyful noise. The ancient Egyptian jubilee fell after a pharaoh had ruled for 30 years, and was repeated every three years thereafter. It was designed to reinvigorate the ruler, giving them a dose of strength and energy.

• THE Queen was born at 17 Bruton Street, London, W1, on April 21, 1926.

• THE Queen was christened Elizabeth Alexandra Mary in the private chapel at Buckingham Palace. She was named after her mother, while her two middle names are those of her paternal great-grandmother, Queen Alexandra, and paternal grandmother, Queen Mary.

• QUEEN Victoria was the last, and to date, the only British monarch to celebrate a diamond jubilee. The Queen, who will be 85 on Accession Day in 2012, will be the oldest monarch to celebrate a diamond jubilee. Queen Victoria was 77 when she celebrated hers in 1897. At that time, the British Empire was at its peak, comprising a quarter of the world's population.

• THE Queen is the only person in Britain who can drive without a licence or a registration number on her car. And she doesn't have a passport.

• IT isn't true that the Queen doesn't carry money. She does once a week - for the collection in church. It's 'a folded note of unknown denomination'.

• THE Queen is the only British monarch in history properly trained to change a spark plug.

• UNUSUAL live gifts given to the monarch on foreign tours include: two tortoises presented in the Seychelles in 1972; a seven-year-old bull elephant called Jumbo from the president of Cameroon in 1972 to mark the Queen's silver wedding anniversary; and two black beavers presented after a visit to Canada.

• THE first royal walkabout took place during the visit by the monarch and Philip to Australia and New Zealand in 1970. The practice was introduced to allow them to meet as many people as possible, not simply officials and dignitaries.

• EVERY day, 200-300 (and sometimes many more) letters from the public arrive. The Queen chooses a selection to read herself and tells members of her staff how she would like them to be answered.

• HER reign in numbers: 3,500 Acts of Parliament; 12 prime ministers; 6 Archbishops of Canterbury; 6 popes; 261 royal overseas visits; 3.5 million letters sent; 45,000 Christmas Cards sent; 175,000 centenarian telegrams sent; 404,500 honours awarded; 58 Queen's Speeches; 129 portraits painted; 30 godchildren; 30 corgis.

Summer Edition 2012

Astronomers moonstruck

Moon brightens up the spring night sky

DURING May the Jersey Astronomy Club held a Question and Answer evening, where members asked a wide range of questions, and Martin Ahier and Tony Isherwood gave replies, and there was a lively discussion.

One of the topics most in the news has been the "super moon" noted in newspapers. This was because the moon's orbit around the earth is not circular, but elliptical. At its closest - "perigee" - it is 221,000 miles from the centre of the Earth, and at its furthest - "apogee" - it is 253,000 miles.

If the moon is full at perigee, it can be 30 times brighter, hence the "super moon". However because the eye takes in more light at night, the difference is not actually that noticeable to the naked eye.

Other topics included the way in which weather patterns of other planets like Jupiter can improve our understanding of Earth's weather, whether the Chinese will have a moonbase in the next 10 years, the wobble in the Earth's axis, and why Galileo thought Saturn had "jug ears" - it was because his telescope was not powerful enough to see the rings.

Tony Isherwood also spoke on how sailors used to make use of a sextant lined up with the sun and horizon by day, and the pole star by night to navigate, and plot their position on the chart.

Diving into the past

Police once went to great depths to secure evidence!

THIS May saw the States of Jersey Police celebrate 60 years of policing in the Island. Policing has changed over the years, and back in the 1970s and 1980s, the police had their own diving unit, which can be seen here in St Brelade's Bay.

Inspector Harry Carré, then a young officer, was the last member to join in 1986, and remembers that they needed six training dives a year. It was important to train all year round.

The purpose of the diving unit was to be able to search reservoirs or rocky gullies offshore for missing people, or for stolen goods dumped in reservoirs. Training took place both in Val de La Mare reservoir, and in the sea. There are a number of wrecks off Jersey's coasts, such as the 'Schokland', a Dutch freighter that sank after hitting a reef in 1943 under the command of German forces; she sits on the sea-bed about a mile off Portelet Bay, at a depth of 20 to 30 metres depending on the tides. Inspector Carré remembers diving into the deep, murky waters to visit the 225 feet long wreck, which can still be seen today by keen wreck divers.

The call for the specialist services of the diving team were infrequent, and in 1988 it was disbanded as uneconomical. Any diving that was required thereafter was handed over to the Harbours Department.

West Show to Wet Show

But nonetheless still 'Singing in the Rain'

ON Saturday, the Acappela Brass Band were playing a lively rendition of "Singing in the Rain", as the rain came down. But people turned up, despite the inclement weather, in good spirits, with wellington boots splashing in the mud, and brollies unfurled.

The finer weather on Sunday saw an upsurge in numbers, and over the two day event, nearly 10,000 people came to enjoy the events and attractions.

While some of the outside attractions were rained off on Saturday, there was still much to see inside the tents, where there were stalls such as the WI,Â the Jersey Privateers Gaming Club with two model sets, Jersey In Transition, with a display of local organic food, and the Durrell stall on the rainforest, where children could handle large beetles. More children's entertainment was provided by a magician in the Chicano Magic Show. Older children could enjoy table tennis.

There was also plenty of tasty food to enjoy such as Genuine Jersey produce, spit-roasts, crepes, hamburgers and hot-dogs, as well as Jersey ice-cream and Jersey wonders, candyfloss and speciality coffees.

The main arena saw the three headline acts well attended "" the Diggerland Dancing Diggers Stunt Team, and the Rockin' Horse Productions Equestrian Stunt Team, and Cyril the Squirrel and his racing terriers.

Mindful of the farming roots of the show, as well as a traditional cattle show, there was a large marquee devoted to Horticultural displays, showcasing a schools carrot growing competition (in conjunction with the Jersey Farmers' Union), the Jersey Rosarians annual rose show, a Jersey Young Farmers stand, and an Allotments stand, promoting the growing local passion for allotments.

Autumn Edition 2012

Green menace returns

A garnish we could do without!

THIS summer has seen a huge build up of green sea lettuce in St. Aubin's Bay. The problem was not helped by the decision in June to stop removing it. However, at the end of August, Transport and Technical Services sent beach cleaning vehicles to remove the sea lettuce, and bury it down by the low tide mark.

St. Brelade businesses claim to have suffered as a result of this policy. Collette's Cabin at La Haule, told La Baguette that the rotting smell had put visitors off, and when wet, the lettuce was quite slippery and hazardous; they had been unable to put benches out on the sand.

Further down the beach, a concessionaire said that when the sea lettuce dried, it turned white, and a number of visitors thought it was toilet paper from a sewage outlet. And, 'Save Our Shorelin'e told La Baguette: "Sea lettuce belongs to the green algae group, grows rapidly and dies off in summer. When it washes up on the beach and begins to decompose, it sometimes smells like sewage, and filmy leaves can be mistaken for toilet paper. It requires relatively plentiful nitrogen and grows primarily in shallow areas that are relatively protected from waves and have good exposure to sunlight. Nitrogen comes from farmland fertiliser, which flows off the land into the bay, especially during the wet weather this summer."

Autumn Edition 2012

Battle success again!

More awards in 2012 for Battle of Flowers team
by Jeff Hathaway and Tony Bellows

ST. Brelade Battle of Flowers had a fantastic Battle this year with their entry "Shangri-La" scooping the Grand Prix des Pariosses Trophy given for being the 3rd best float on The Avenue, just behind the Prix d'Honnuer and the Prix d'Excellence.

The Association also received the Best Set Piece Award and the Best Costume Award this being the third time they have received this award in the past four years. Committee member Janet Le Gros told La Baguette: "A big thank you must go to our costume maker Yvonne Binet for all her hard work. Our 'thank you' list is enormous from the Chairman down to the catering staff and everyone who gave their time and effort to help us complete this fantastic entry. We must also thank our designers Simon Thomas and Nigel Gates for their stunning design. We would also like to take this opportunity to thank all those parishioners who took the time to send in donations to help us enter into the Parade. We are always looking for help with the float, so please feel free to com to the shed to meet us and join in."

But there is a lot of hard work behind the float as La Baguette found out.

Planning for the Battle of Flowers begins early. During November 2011, the St Brelade's Battle of Flowers Association met to discuss ideas for the design of the float for the 2012 Battle of Flowers.

By December, Shangri-La was chosen, and materials ordered for the framework. By May 2012, the framework is mostly in place, built around the chassis of a refuse lorry. Hares tails were being glued to separated sections, and underlying frame painted.

With suitable music chosen, the trained dancers begin rehearsing their routines. But the big rush comes in the four nights before the Battle itself, when many volunteers young and old arrive and 130,000 heads are glued to the float together with 80 kilos of hares tails.

The Chairman of the Association, Michael Jandron, gets an early night around 10.30 on the eve before the Battle. Early around 5 o'clock on the Battle morning, he is in the driving seat, an enclosed and very hot and noisy place inside the structure.

Directions are given to him over headphones from two people walking beside the float, and he has a tiny camera mounted at the front, which enables him to see the white line in the centre of the road. At five miles an hour, the float creeps down Beaumont Hill to the Battle Arena, where in early afternoon, the Battle magic begins once more.

Autumn Edition 2012

Parishioners Remember: St Aubin's Fete

Joy Oxenden remembers Portelet Holiday Camp and St. Aubin Fete

THE St Aubin's Fete and Water Carnival ran for many years, ending in the late 1960s due to increased traffic in the St. Aubin's village. Taking place two weeks after the Battle of Flowers, the smaller fairground stalls relocated to St Aubin on the land behind the Parish Hall. There was a parade, with fancy dress costumes, bands playing, and a procession of the smaller Battle of Flowers floats.

During the post-war period, Joy Oxenden lived at the Jersey Holiday Camp at Portelet, run at that time by her father, Major Nigel Oxenden until his death in 1948, after which his wife Pat took over the running of the Holiday Camp. Joy has lots of memories of the entries by the Holiday Camp in the Battle of Flowers, which would later see a second appearance in the St Aubin's Fete.

"Holiday makers would come to stay and work on the float every year, deciding among themselves during the Winter on the design", she remembered. "We had an entry under Section K for Hotels. Then two weeks later, when the St Aubin Fete was on, another group of holiday makers would come over and take the float there too.

Sometimes there would also be an entry in the Water Carnival which took place in St Aubin's harbour. They would often dress up in costumes suitable for the theme of the float.

One year was rather risqué for its time with a title of "Heavenly Bodies" which was based on the Planets, with young people dressed accordingly as to the Gods & Goddesses they represented, you can imagine how this was turned into funny jokes!"

She remembers how the visitors loved to return to the camp at their particular time during the season. "It was always the same people, year after year, who enjoyed The Battle of Flowers and looked forward to participation in the events as the main feature of their holiday experience."

Autumn Edition 2012

Picture of health

Harbour Gallery celebrates 10 years, 'but time to move' on says co-director, Pat Robson

THE Harbour Gallery began 10 years ago when Pat Robson and Elizabeth Le Gal were looking for somewhere to showcase local artistic talent. With a background as art teachers, they had founded a charity, Art in the Framework Foundation, to put on art and craft workshops and hold exhibitions. Finding premises for exhibitions for longer than three weeks was difficult, until the opportunity suddenly arose to take on the lease of their current premises.

With the aid of a grant from the Tourism Development Fund, they took downstairs and one room upstairs, and set up The Harbour Gallery. This enabled exhibitions to be showcased all year round. Further space became available upstairs, and in 2005, the relocation off-island by a finance company who used much of upstairs for archive storage meant they could expand to have a café and a permanent location for workshops, as well as additional studio space.

The aim of The Harbour Gallery is to support and showcase new local artists and craft workers, rather than well established commercial artists. The studio spaces have been full from day one. There are a wide variety of workshop events - for example, ones run by Mencap, artists textile group, indigo dying, and half-term and holidays are especially popular for children's workshops. There's an enthusiastic team of volunteers, but the forward planning for events is done by Pat and Elizabeth about six months in advance.

Every year there are 10 major exhibitions, and the Jersey Textile Showcase, which runs in March, sees hundreds of people coming from the UK and Europe for a week, with local hotels and restaurants benefiting from the visitors.

A question mark hangs over the future of the gallery, as both Pat and Elizabeth are retiring at the end of the year. A new organiser need to be found to manage The Harbour Gallery, although the volunteers and workshop providers will remain to help with the day to day operational duties. It is hoped that such a worthwhile enterprise will continue, as it provides local employment, a venue on the Tourism map, and a much needed outlet for local arts and crafts.

However, events have been fully booked for the future, and a date for the diary is participation in the Genuine Jersey Christmas event, running in the Gallery from the 29th November to 2nd of December this year.

Autumn Edition 2012

Bella Vista!

Murray's golden Labrador

YOU may have seen Parishioner Murray Treanor and his distinctive Labrador, Bella, out on the pavements on St Brelade. Murray is blind, and Bella is a specially trained Guide Dog for the Blind.

Murray had always problems with his sight, but this was not fully diagnosed until he was 14, when he was sent to a school in the UK especially for the blind or partially sighted. His loss of sight is a degenerative condition, and for many years he thought he could manage, and held out against having a guide dog. But he has now had two, the first, Elton, has been retired, and now Bella who is 2½ years old, and he says he wouldn't be without them.

Dogs are trained as puppies, with six months intensive training, and then trained in socialisation over a period of two years, part of which is with their new owner. The Guide Dogs for The Blind endeavours to match dog to owner, and the owner's lifestyle. Murray had to go to the UK for training, and also come back with an instructor to check familiar and important routes - "the bus stop, the football club, and the pub', he says, tongue in cheek. Bella goes on the bus with Murray and has a special basket to lie in at work.

The popular "biggest" book sale for the Guide Dogs for the Blind Association will be held on 20th and 21st October at the RJ&HS Showground in Trinity, and Murray hopes that Parishioners from St Brelade will support this worthy cause.

Autumn Edition 2012

Gig in the garden

Garden event raises money for charity

THERE was plenty of musical entertainment from young people at "The Gig in the Garden" which took place in August at Reg's Garden.

The event was organised by Hautlieu student Alex Andrews, and local musical talent played all day including Syn3rgy, Salems Lot (pictured above) and many solo performers. Music was performed on a variety of instruments, including drums, guitars and keyboards. The last band to take the stage were Alfresco Bandits, who went on to achieve notable success in the Battle of the Bands and appeared at Jersey Live. There was also a raffle, a BBQ and a cake sale.

The event raised a magnificent £1959.87 for Teenage Cancer Trust which will go to help with research, facilities and setting up games consoles, plasma screen televisions, Sky TV, and games rooms so that patients can interact with each other and relax as much as they can.

Autumn Edition 2012

On another planet!

Astronomy Club discuss Curiousity

THE Jersey Astronomy Club met at the Patrick Moore Centre on September 10th at 8.00 p.m. to discuss Mars, the Curiosity Rover and literature on Mars through the ages.

In 1877, the astronomer Giovanni Schiaparelli observed what he thought were canals on the surface of Mars, and the astronomer Percival Lowell suggested that an advanced but desperate culture had built the canals to tap Mars' polar ice caps, the last source of water on an inexorably drying planet. Better astronomical studies showed the canals were an optical illusion caused by poor quality telescope views. But primitive life may have existed.

On Earth, the earliest record of microbial life dates back 3.5 billion years, the same time scientists believe Mars was wet and warm. Over the next two years, the NASA Curiosity Rover will explore the Martian landscape for signs of water and microbial life in the geological history of the planet.

Autumn Edition 2012

January sails!

New bus company and new livery for 2013

JERSEY'S new buses will feature sails and the names of parishes in Jérriais. CT Plus, the new bus operators from January 2013, put forward two designs in a public poll, and the sails design received 80% of the vote. La Baguette's roving reporter went out to gauge the reaction of St Brelade Parishioners to the design.

"It's nice and bright and cheerful, and I like the Parish names across it."
"I'm glad they have the Jérriais names of Parishes. There should be more use of Jérriais around the Island.'
"It's a much better design that the 'flying banana' logo."
"It's good notjust to have plain white."
"I like the Parish crests hidden within the sails."
"It will brighten up the dark days of January."

And former Constable Mike Jackson, past Minister at TTS, said "Speaking as a nautical person, I think it is a very apposite design for a summer seaside resort."

Autumn Edition 2012

Jumbo size repairs!

Elephant slides off for refurbishment

A little girl, playing in the Elephant Park, told her mother, with impeccable logic, that 'it shouldn't be called the elephant park anymore because it doesn't have an elephant there".

La Baguette's reporter asked mothers for their children's reactions, and found that a large number were still asking where the elephant had gone. St Brelade's elephant slide has in fact been sent for repairs and will be returning later this year. A safety report noted that the fibreglass had some cracks and chips.

Constable Steve Pallet said: "I've been joking to people that she's gone off to the vets. But as we do every year, we had a report done by a company that shows us what safety requirements are needed. The elephant was chipped and had some slight cracks so we agreed to get it repaired."

The elephant, originally donated by Reg Langlois, currently has no name, but plans are afoot to give it one. Well known elephants include Nellie the Elephant, Elmer the Elephant and Barbar the Elephant. So, what name should St Brelade's Elephant be given?

Write to La Baguette c/o St. Brelade Parish Hall, Le Neuve Route, St. Aubin, St. Brelade, Jersey JE3 8BS with your suggestions.

Autumn Edition 2012

Recipe Corner: 'Ortchie' - a traditional Jersey soup

"ORTCHIE", or stinging nettle soup, is an intrinsic Jersey dish that only fell out of favour a generation ago. It was also a staple part of the diet for Islander and German alike during the German Occupation It is a humble, and nutritional dish well worth reviving.

Make sure that only young leaves are used as the older they become the harder it is to break down the silica that makes up the stinging parts of the leaf. Keep your eye out throughout the late summer and autumn, though, because young crops of freshly seeded nettles will grow wherever and whenever they get a chance. Here's one recipe:

INGREDIENTS
1 pint young nettle leaves
2 pints meat stock
2 ozs, fine oatmeal
2 ozs. butter
salt and pepper

METHOD
Wash nettle leaves and chop.
Melt butter in saucepan and saut%eacute; oatmeal until brown and crisp. Then add stock and seasoning, bring to boil, stirring occasionally and simmer for 10 minutes.

Add nettle leaves and cook for a further 5 minutes.

Serve with a dab of butter in warmed bowls with plenty of hot dry toast to dip in.

This is a delicious and very economical recipe. Don't use old nettles that have gone to seed or even in flower, and if you have plenty of them use the tops only. (Don't forget to wear rubber gloves whilst picking and preparing them!) It will please all health food conscious and natural whole food fans, particularly if served with 100% wholemeal toast.

Bouon Appetit!

Autumn Edition 2012

Harbour Gallery top ten Lieutenant Governor opens 10th Birthday Exhibition

WELL over 100 people attended the opening of the Harbour Gallery's 10th Birthday Exhibition on the 8th of November, which displayed a selection of work of local artists spanning the ten years of the Gallery's existence.

It was officially opened by the Lieutenant Governor, His Excellency General Sir John McColl and his wife Lady McColl. Sir John said how one of the first things he and his wife did when they arrived in Jersey was to visit the Harbour Gallery, and they had returned many times since.

He had originally tried to work out what exactly it was, as they walked around. Was it an exhibition centre, an arts shop, a place for workshops, an educational place for schools and young people, a studio, a place for local artists, or a place where overseas artists would come, or simply a venue for people to come and chat and drink tea?

It was, he said, all of these things, or at least had become over time, all of these things. It had grown over a ten year period, with initiative and energy of Islanders in supporting the Gallery, fuelled by the imagination of local artists, and the volunteers who made it such a welcoming place to visit.

From its origins in Art in the Frame, 14 years ago, to the Harbour Gallery of today, he said that it would not have happened were it not for the hard work and dedication of two people, above all, who stuck by their vision and made it happen "" co-founders Pat Robson and Elizabeth Le Gal.

After his speech, Pat Robson thanked him, and thanked those artists who had contributed so much over the last 10 years, all those who had volunteered their time, and those who had visited and supported the Gallery, some of whom had been with the Gallery since its inception. Finally, Lady McColl cut the celebratory birthday cake, and those present applauded.

Autumn Edition 2012

Who's behind Christmas? The secret is out - but mum's the word

by Guest Reporter, Monty Le Brun

You always hear about Father Christmas around December, but spare a thought for Mother Christmas, who often doesn't get much of a mention. She's the one who actually goes out and buys all the presents. Men don't like shopping, and Santa is no exception, I'm afraid. Wrestling through the shopping crowds to find those perfect gifts is not one of his skills.

And then she has to wrap them all up neatly. Like many men, that's not a skill that Father Christmas has ever acquired. If he had to wrap anything up, it would be a shapeless mess, girded with lashings of sticky tape. But Mother Christmas knows how. She's gone through eight thousand rolls of sticky tape and one million metres of gift wrap, all so that it will be ready for him to deliver on Christmas Eve.

So there Father Christmas is, stretched out, as you see him in the Christmas card, his rosy cheeks and beaming smile, eating mince pies beside a roaring fire. If a camera could pan around the room, you'd see Mother Christmas neatly cutting paper, placing bows and ribbons on all the presents, ticking them off the list. Her other skills include her duties baking those mince pies and washing Father Christmas' socks.

In a moment, she'll rouse him from his slumber, and put his freshly cleaned red lined fur coat on, give him the sack and send him on his way. And with a yo-ho-ho, his sleigh will lift off into the night sky, and he'll deliver all those presents, prepared earlier by Mother Christmas. All he has to do is to work hard one night of the year. No wonder Father Christmas looks so happy when you see him!

Christmas Edition 2012

Body of influence - Planning Group begin to examine recent applications

THE St. Brelade Planning Group, formed earlier this year, have over the last two months been examining various planning applications in the Parish.

Group Chairman Pauline Paintin told La Baguette that she and her team had been pleased to note that the majority of proposed schemes they have looked at were well-designed and 'thought-through' offering little in the way of criticism. She said: "Regrettably there are a small number of proposals that have found little favour with the group members or the residents most closely affected and bodies such as the National Trust. They relate largely to coastal and shoreline locations where the consensus is that the projects proposed are considerably 'out of context' and raise many questions in with regard to altering the character of the area. Parishioners as a whole are becoming more aware of developments in St. Brelade irrespective of whether they're on their doorstep or not."

"The group concede that in these early days of its formation it is still finding it's feet although it has already built a good rapport with many developers and the Planning Department." She said. Group spokesman Jeff Hathaway said: "We are particularly concerned with some of the current developments proposed for St. Brelades Bay and St. Aubin. These two important areas have been highlighted in the Island Plan as requiring 'special consideration'. However, as yet supplementary guidelines have not been drawn up.

The result is the continuation of piecemeal development that is beginning to compromise the traditional and historic character of both."

The Group told La Baguette that it was not formed to oppose development, but to influence the future shape of the Parish through consultation with residents and all parties to development schemes to find the most favourable and appropriate solutions and foster a process that avoids conflict.

The group are on the look out for more members and particularly a Minutes Secretary. If you feel you could give some of your time and have an interest in shaping future development in the Parish, please contact Chairman Pauline Paintin by email: cavokjersey@gmail.com

Christmas Edition 2012

Mud, mud, glorious mud: St. Aubin's Harbour gets a clean out

by **Guest Reporter, Kay Bisson**

THE dredging of St Aubin's harbour commenced in early October and is anticipated to take about four months to complete.

The decision to dredge over the autumn and winter, outside of the summer holiday season, was taken after consultation with St Aubin's Boat Owner's Association and to minimise disruption to harbour users, residents and St. Aubin businesses.

The majority of the mud and silt removed from the harbour will be taken by road to La Collette with the remainder loaded onto a barge to be disposed of at sea in a licensed area some 4 miles south of the Island.

Work will be carried out during weekdays and, while there is likely to be some noise disruption, weekend or night work is not planned although the works need to scheduled around suitable tidal and weather conditions.

Christmas Edition 2012

Parishioners Remember Peter Turley remembers his time in Bomber Command

THE Bomber Command Memorial was unveiled in London in June this year by the Queen, a belated recognition of the significant part that bombers played in World War II with their raids on Germany's industrial heartland.

Peter Turley, who is now resident at Maison St Brelade, was a young man of 21 when he was rear gunner on a Lancaster on those flights. He made 34 operational flights over Germany, and bailed out once over Belgium. He said.

"I will be thinking about those times today. The memorial is a bit late in coming, but it's great that we now have the memorial to remember the bomber crews." He enjoyed the visit to London, and said 'it was very well organised, and spoke to HRH the Duchess of Cornwall, Camilla.'

The night flights were long, sometimes lasting 8 or 9 hours. "I was scared most of the time as we all were," said Peter, "but I kept alert." Once they had passed through particularly intense of flak, and then one single flak burse hit the aircraft just 100 yards behind them. He saw a big black explosion, and the plane began a spiral descent while he watched, hoping the crew would bail out. The spiral grew faster, but no one left the stricken craft, which broke into two as it plunged down.

The memorial in London was both to those who survived, and those who lost their lives. The crew that Peter was with made it through the war. They were all volunteers, making dangerous flights to attack German armament factories. It is often forgotten how young these men were, mostly around 18 to 22, with an older skipper of 31. It is right and proper that they should be remembered with a memorial today.

Christmas Edition 2012

Heroic airmen commemorated

by Ian Le Sueur and Tony Bellows

IT is 70 years since the fateful flight of No 600 Squadron. In 1942, the unit was operating from Warmwell to the Cotentin Peninsula and Channel Islands.

The Squadron concentrated on anti-shipping patrols, often 'scrambled' to attack convoys moving between the Channel Islands or coming out of Cherbourg, and they sunk two coastal ships off the coast of Alderney.

At 13.10 on December 7, 1942 eight Whirlwinds departed Warmwell on a low level anti-shipping strike. Squadron Leader R S Woodward led Red section of four aircraft, and Flying Officer Lovell led Blue section. The weather was grey and windy. An enemy convoy was sighted south-west of Jersey lying just off St Brelade Bay. The two anti flak units went in first, closely followed by Red section, led by Woodward. They attacked two vessels of 800 and 500 tons. Woodward's bombs over-shot, but Sergeant Williams, flying as Red Two, scored a direct on the larger vessel and set it on fire.

But disaster struck Woodward's aircraft. The intense flak damaged his aircraft and he was seen making a controlled landing 400 yards from the nearest vessel. Blue section attacked next but Blue Three, Canadian Warrant Officer Donald McPhail, flew into a flak burst and disappeared straight into the sea.

No news was ever received of Woodward and it became apparent that he too had been lost in the forced landing of his aircraft.

A memorial to Woodward and McPhail was erected at Noirmont, in remembrance of these brave airman who lost their lives.

Christmas Edition 2012

On a different planet: Breaking through the clouds of Venus

by Guest Reporter, Monty Croix

THE Jersey Astronomy Club met at the Patrick Moore Centre on November 12th 10th at 8:00 p.m. to listen to a talk on "Astronomy and Science Fiction: Venus" (which some scholars believe to be the Star of Bethlehem), given by Tony Bellows.

He explained how early science fiction was driven by Laplace's Nebular Hypothesis, a theory of how the Solar System came into being from a swirling cloud of interstellar dust pulled together by gravity. Laplace's scheme had the planets close to the sun as being in a younger, more primitive state than Earth, and those further out as older, more ancient.

This was illustrated by extracts from science fiction writers on the planet Venus, with its cloud cover suggesting a watery humid landscape, like the prehistoric Earth. Writers covered included Edgar Rice Burroughs, Robert Heinlein, C.S. Lewis, Isaac Asimov and John Wyndham.

The talk ended by looking at the very different picture revealed by the Mariner 2 space probe of 1962, which showed Venus was an inhospitable planet with a surface temperature of over 462 C.

Christmas Edition 2012

Christmas trivia Now, not a lot of people know that!

by Michael Le Quesne

• One of the most popular Christmas songs, "Jingle Bells" was actually written in 1857 for America's Thanksgiving Day. Composed by James Pierpont, it was originally called "One-Horse Open Sleigh."

• Pope Julius I declared December 25th as the official day for Christmas in the fourth century. In 529 AD, the Emperor Justinian declared Christmas a civic holiday.

• Germany made the first artificial Christmas trees during the 19th century. They were made of goose feathers and dyed green.

• "Silent Night" was written in 1818, by an Austrian pastor, Joseph Mohr. As Christmas Eve came, that year, the organ in his church was broken, so together with his friend, Franz Gruber, he wrote this new tune - and played it on his guitar.

• The abbreviation-Xmas for Christmas is thought by some to be sacreligious, but in fact the first letter of the Greek word for Christ is chi, which is X.

• If you received all of the gifts in the song "The Twelve Days of Christmas," you would receive 364 gifts.

• In 1843, "A Christmas Carol" was written by Charles Dickens in just six weeks.

• During the ancient 12-day Christmas celebration, the log burned was called the "Yule log." Sometimes a piece of the Yule log would be kept to kindle the fire the following winter, to ensure that the good luck carried on from year to year. The Yule log custom was handed down from the Druids.

• There are two Christmas Islands. One in the Pacific Ocean formerly called Kiritimati and Christmas Island in the Indian Ocean.

• In 1752, 11 days were dropped from the year when the switch from the Julian calendar to the Gregorian calendar was made -December 25 effectively moved 11 days backwards

• In Britain, eating mince pies at Christmas dates back to the 16th century. It is still believed that to eat a mince pie on each of the Twelve Days of Christmas will bring 12 happy months in the year to follow.

• In France, Christmas is called Noel. This is derived from the French phrase "les bonnes nouvelles," which means literally "the good news" and refers to the gospel.

• In the British armed forces it is traditional that officers wait on their men and serve them their Christmas dinner. This dates back to a custom from the Middle Ages.

• It is a British Christmas tradition that a wish made while mixing the Christmas pudding will come true only if the ingredients are stirred in a clockwise direction.

• The custom of singing Christmas carols is very old - the earliest English collection was published in 1521

• It is estimated that 400,000 people become sick each year from eating tainted Christmas leftovers.

• The first British monarch to broadcast a Christmas message to his people was King George V. Queen Elizabeth's Christmas message to the nation was televised for the first time on December 25, 1957.

Festive Recipe Corner A Victorian recipe and just a bit different !

by Clodagh Sarb

AROUND the 1950s, the Wessex and Jersey Branch of the National Association of Flower Arrangement Societies brought out a fund raising recipe book. There's an easily prepared recipe in the book for Boxing Day which was provided by the Chairman at the time, Mrs Nora Alldridge.

She comments "This is a Victorian recipe from my grandmother, which no doubt did much to dispel the excesses of Christmas Day. My sons swear it is essential on the menu if they are to survive and enjoy New Year's Eve!"

Ingredients:
12 ozs. Prunes
4 ozs. split almonds
1 blackcurrant jelly
whipped cream to decorate

Method:
Soak prunes overnight, then simmer until tender. Reserve juice and cut prunes in half, removing stones. Dissolve jelly in half pint water. Cool until almost set then add prunes and juice and place in mould to set. Remove from mould and decorate with almonds and whipped cream.

Christmas Edition 2012

Yule like this! A light hearted look at the events of the year - to a well known tune:

I'm dreaming of a light Christmas
Just like the ones I used to know
No JEC cable breaking
And power cut making
To leave us freezing in the snow

I'm dreaming of a blue Christmas
Royal blue, and flags a waving
Beacon from Noirmont see ablazing
Jubilee we had such celebrating

I'm dreaming of a yellow Christmas,
Jogging with the Olympic Torch, I go
Past the Elephant in the Park
It really is such a lark
To run with trainers in the snow

I'm dreaming of a green Christmas
Sea lettuce on beaches, such a blight
A letter to the JEP, I think I'll write
And may all your seaweed be out of sight

I'm dreaming of a white Christmas
Just like the ones I used to know.
La Baguette will still deliver
Even if cold winds make us shiver
Merry Christmas and Ho, Ho, Ho!

Fun and Games

St. Brelade to host Twinning Games Saturday 8th June

THE Twinning Games (or "Jeux inter- Jumelage" as they are called in France) are to be hosted by St. Brelade in 2013 and will be held on Saturday 8th June at Les Quennevais Playing Fields.

The games will comprise of around 12 competitors from each of the participating Jersey parishes and their French twin counterparts. Connétable Pallett described the games as an 'It's a Knockout' style of competition, played largely for fun. He said: "While there will be serious competition with winners and losers in all events, its more about participating and having a good laugh and establishing ever stronger bonds with our twinning partners. The last games were a huge success - so many new friends made - I'm really looking forward to the weekend."

The 'games' will be officially opened at 10.30 by the Bailiff . The Opening Ceremony features each team carrying their Parish and Normandy town banner in a parade around the arena area.

This year the games will consist of 7 or 8 events, depending on time factors, played in the main arena. The teams will consist of 12 competitors each with 11 parish teams taking part in a combination of 6 from each parish and their twinned town. From thereon each event is a straight knockout competition. From attendance figures at past games it is anticipated there to be at least a 1,000 supporters and public spectators to cheer on the teams.

Refreshments will be available from either the Café des Sport in the main sports centre who will also be providing a catering van located close to the arena offering light-refreshments, snacks and drinks. St. John Ambulance will also be in attendance to provide first aid, if needed, for both competitors and spectators. Parking will be in Les Quennevais Sports Centre main car parks in front and behind the main building. As a contingency, overspill parking will be provided on the sports field itself, but not until the main car park becomes full. Marshalls and Honorary Police will be directing traffic in and around the venue.

Julian Bernstein told La Baguette: "St. Brelade have competed in previous games held in both Jersey and Normandy. They were tremendous fun and just as entertaining to watch as to take part - it really is a great event! St. Brelade have built a fantastic relationship with our twin town of Granville. We are very proud to be hosting the games this year which I hope will be the best ever!"

The St. Brelade team has yet to be finalised and there are still one or two places left. Constable Pallett told La Baguette: "Participation is not just about being part of the team , but we also need a variety of helpers, of all ages, to make sure the event runs smoothly. There are many small but no less important details that we need help with - so if you would like to help out the Twinning Association or Parish Hall would be delighted to hear from you."

St. Brelade Twinning Association Chairman, Julian Bernstein together with his team have been busy organising the activities and a provisional timetable has now been drawn up for this all-day family event. Competitions are to include: Waiters and Waitresses Race, Caterpillar Race, Jersey and French flags Puzzle Game, Bat the Wheel and Dress the Scarecrow...and more

The teams from France and their supporters will be arriving on the ferry at 9.00 am, and the athletes and team manager will be taken to Les Quennevais Sports Centre for breakfast.

A website has been set up with details of this and other future Twinning Association events at http://jerseynormandie.com. The St. Brelade Twinning Association can be contacted on 746353 or Trish Davey at the Parish Hall on 741141 if you are interested in participating as a competitor or helper.

Easter Edition 2013

Parish plug shortfall Solution to avoid drain on municipal resources

by Guest Reporter, Pauline Legge

THE harbour at St Aubin's is full of boats once more, now that dredging operations have been completed. The sharp-eyed viewer may notice that the harbour, when full at high tide, now remains one yard below its previous high water mark. (See picture).

In a leaked report, La Baguette has learned that in the course of dredging the mud away, some historic damage to the harbour floor was uncovered.

Older members of St Aubin's community may remember that here is a vast circular cast iron plug, about 3 yards in diameter, which was made to keep extra water in the harbour to enable larger boats to moor. This appears to have been damaged at some time in the past.

The first plug was made of solid oak in Elizabethan times, when Sir Walter Raleigh deemed "forsooth the waters should be retained, privy for the berth of larger vessels of trade". The money was raised by a levy on the rates.

In Victorian times, the oak was badly rotting, and the Connétable stated that "des centaines de livres sont parties en fumée". A cast iron plug was made to replace it, by ironmongers, again financed by the rates.

Repairs to this plug are therefore needed, and a special early assembly of the Parish is planned for April 1st to levy an emergency increase on the Parish rates of 1p to pay for it. After the assembly, which will be held at 11 am, there will be a traditional fish breakfast of "poisson d'avril".

Easter Edition 2013

Cold snap! No planning application required!

THIS year, snow blizzards in March caused major disruption to traffic, bringing brought down trees and settling into deep drifts. A as result, schools were closed, giving a bonus school holiday to children.

Snow is very much a part of childhood; for the child, it is an enchanted wonderland, where the hedgerows and rooftops are painted white, as if by magic. Parents grumble, but the child becomes, for a short while, a polar explorer. It is a time of simple joy. They can build a snowman, or have a snow fight, or even make an igloo! Picture. Left to right: Mischa Bailey, Callum Wedgberg and Alex Noel with their igloo at Quennevais Park

Easter Edition 2013

Quennevais masterplan

Packed Communicare discusses proposed improvements

OVER one hundred parishioners attended a meeting at Communicare on the 8th March to hear proposals for the Parish to take responsibility for carparks, footpaths, and green areas round Les Quennevais and Clos des Sable - currently the responsibility of Jersey Property Holdings (JPH). Chaired by the Constable, Steve Pallett, also there to answer questions were Philip Ahier and Ray Foster of JPH, Deputy Eddie Noel, Assistant Treasury Minister, Deputy Montfort Tadier and Deputy John Young.

Constable Steve Pallett explained that the meeting was to gauge the opinion of the residents before taking firm proposals to a Parish Assembly. The current situation was that the Parish was unable to police parts of the area, or initiate residential parking schemes in these areas. It would also potentially enable residents to convert part of their gardens to provide parking if required. The land in question would become the responsibility of the Parish, but only after Jersey Property Holdings had done remedial work on some areas of tarmac. The potential cost to the Parish would be maintenance of green areas, and he would provide estimates for the Parish Assembly. Deputy Tadier added that it was a pragmatic solution, which would allow the Parish to intervene in traffic and parking problems.

Questions were raised about costs and whether they would be born by ratepayers. Constable Pallett said there would be a cost, but the remedial work on roads before transfer of ownership would reduce the liability. Deputy John Young said that unless there was a transfer and proper management, nothing would be happen, and residents frustrations would continue; only the local community could effect change.

A show of hands was called and was unanimous in favour of progressing matters to a Parish Assembly, which will be held at Les Quennevais.

Easter Edition 2013

Gallery Shines! Re-opening is toasted occasion

ON 7 February, the Harbour Gallery re-opened with a "new look", and an exhibition of paintings, textiles and jewellery entitled "Shine". On arrival, visitors were entertained by musician Giles Robson playing blues on his harmonica. Toastmaster David Lister, of the Northern Guild of Toastmasters, gave a formal introduction to Professor Ed Sallis, OBE, the guest speaker. Professor Sallis said that he was "incredibly proud to open the exhibition of the refurbished harbour gallery".

He thanked Elizabeth Le Gal for being one of the co-founders of the Gallery, now part of the team of volunteers, and praised the many volunteers, without whose efforts the Gallery would not be possible; they showed "the great community spirit that existed in Jersey". And he thanked Pat Robson both for deciding to carry on with the Gallery, and also taking it forward with innovations.

"This is the art centre for the West of the Island", he said, and it was opening with a fine exhibition of work from Helena Mundy, Katherine Cadin, Clare Ormsby, Luinda Ranji and Lisa Le Brocq, as well as pictures from international artist Heath Hearn, who exhibited when the Gallery originally began. There was buffet in the newly revamped Cameo Café for visitors to enjoy.

Easter Edition 2013

Confused signs Where or what is Woodford?

HAVE you ever been confused by the sign at the end of the promenade in St Brelade's, just next to the Oyster Box? It informs the public that if these toilets are closed, the nearest available ones are to be found in "Woodford". But where is Woodford?

In 1961, after the death of Mr P. Ellis, a property called "Woodford" in St Brelade's Bay came on the market. Bob Smale, a St Brelade Deputy at the time, put forward a private members proposition for the States to acquire the property and the extensive gardens, and turn them into a park for the benefit of Islanders. This was taken up by the Defense, Tourism and Natural Beauties Committees, whose members all favoured the purchase of the property on behalf of the public of the Island, and the Public Works Committee was assigned the task of negotiating for its purchase.

A letter was received from Mr Vernon Tomes (later to become Deputy Bailiff and Senator) who represented the heirs of the estate, and this confirmed that his clients were prepared to sell the property to the States for the sum of £60,000. The total cost, after legal fees, was £61,000.

The park itself was originally called "Woodford Park", and so remained until 1966, when it was renamed "The Winston Churchill Memorial Park", and it is in the car park adjacent to this park that 'the nearest alternative public toilets' can be found.

Easter Edition 2013

Mammoth task

New sculpture for 2013 unveiled in St. Brelade Bay

ON Saturday the 5th January, a new sculpture designed by Dan Entwhistle entitled "DeNAtured" was unveiled in the hotel garden opposite the entrance to the St Brelade's Bay Hotel. Constructed of steel and resin, in the shape of a mammoth, the piece will remain on its podium for the next year, and be floodlit at night, after which further sculpture will be selected by competition."'''

Speaking at the opening, Stephen Lilley, Chairman of the Podium Art Committee said that they were very pleased with 8 submissions from both emerging talent and established artists, all of which were Jersey based. The competition forms part of the Percent for Art contribution for the new DW Health Club development.

The Constable, Steve Pallett said that he was very pleased with the number of entries, although the very high quality of the entrants made the judges' task extremely difficult. All those who took part could be proud of their submissions. Dan Entwistle's winning entry captured the history of the bay, as it looked out over to La Cotte headland, where Neanderthal man had hunted and eaten woolly mammoths around 100,000 years ago.

34 year old Mr Entwistle told La Baguette that he had always been interested in art from school, and hoped this was the first in a series of Jersey inspired sculptures. He also wished to thank his friend and parishioner Tim Evans who had helped with the construction, which had taken 200 hours to complete.

Parishioners Remember

Caroline Woodhill remembers an expanding post war St. Brelade

IN 1958, Caroline Woodhill came over to Jersey on holiday to stay with her sister who lived in a bungalow near Corbi&eagrave;re. Corbi&eagrave;re still had lighthouse keepers and was not be automated until 1976, and she remembers that her sister was a good friend with one of the keeper's wives.

With her sister, she would visit the nearby Tartan Bar, a favourite stop for coaches on "mystery tours", or the Corbi&eagrave;re Pavilion, now the Corbi&eagrave;re Phare. She enjoyed her stay and came back in 1959 to live in Jersey for good, at Clos des Sables. It was a time of change in St Brelade. Les Quennevais was just being developed: "I remember suddenly more and more houses going up on what had been empty land." Next to La Moye school was La Moye Pub, a venue for folk dancing evenings; further along she remembers St Teresa's Chapel, later demolished to make way for Clos Orange Estate. But by far the most unusual thing she remembers is the airport - "the road to the airport building crossed part of the airport runway, and there were traffic lights, going red as planes came in or took off."

At Red Houses, the R.M. Stores (pictured opposite) was advertised as the "new Western Shopping Centre"; she recalls that "it was a veritable Aladdin's cave, selling anything from butchery, provisions, green grocery, wines and spirits and confectionary to drapery, hardware, glass and china."

Not many people had fridges in the early 1960s, so ingenuity was used: "we used to keep bottles of milk cool by placing them in polystyrene containers outside in the shade". They had no central heating, "only a small paraffin heater and a coal fire. And there were some bitter winters."

She'd also go into town with her friends, and learnt ballroom dancing, which was taught by Mr Brett at Brett's School of Dancing, at the Plaza by West's Cinema.

"The Pavilion at West Park was the place to go on Saturday nights, where there was ballroom dancing, and also rock 'n' roll. Sunday nights would often be a trip to the Odeon cinema with friends to watch the latest films."

But in the summer, when warm, they would take a hamper down to Beauport Bay, and have a picnic. Despite the changes of the 1960s that is still unspoilt, she says, and one of her favourite bays.

Easter Edition 2013

Desert adventure

Team Portside tackle Sahara for charity

AN epic journey began in January for David and Phyllis Pallot as "Team Portside", as they set off in their Unimog from Jersey to take part in the 2013 Intercontinental Rally. The event began in Spain, and they had to drive all the way there from Jersey, after taking the Condor Ferry to France. Taking part at their own expense, they hope to use the publicity from their participation to raise awareness of the Grace Trust, which helps the needy in Jersey, and any donations raised will go 100% towards the trust.

The rally is an annual long distance off-road competition over challenging terrain. It was born two years ago from the dream that amateur racers and adventurers can conquer the Sahara and complete the mythical journey to Dakar. The route passes through some of the most spectacular landscapes in Morocco, Mauritania and Senegal, encompassing the endless dunes of the Sahara, desolate expanses of coastal deserts, the rocky trails of the Atlas mountains, and low lying savannah. It's a journey of some 5,000 km, although Team Portside had an extra 5,000 km extra, driving from Jersey to Spain and back, on the road for 5 weeks.

This year, David and Phyllis joined 139 participants from 11 countries driving 80 cars, motorcycles, quads and trucks. They drove their 1979 Mercedes Unimog, a classic car, which had been made ready for the arduous route with help from Mark Syvret of Romerils. Their journey was also tracked by students of Grainville as part of a geography project, using the spot tracker system.

David & Phyllis are also collecting food (tins, dry food) for distribution to those in need. Items can be left at the Portside Salon at St Aubin along with any donations to the Grace Trust.

Details for making direct donations to the Trust can be found at: www.gracetrust.com/giving_grace_trust_jersey.htm

Easter Edition 2013

Bang in the night Prof. Andy Newsam visits Jersey

ON 18th December, the Jersey Astronomy Club were pleased to host a talk by Andy Newsom, Professor of Astronomy Education and Engagement at the Liverpool John Moores University and also the director of the National Schools Observatory.

After an introduction by John Tarrant of Education, who had arranged the event, Professor Newsom gave a talk entitled "Things that go bang in the night". With great enthusiasm, he talked about the Liverpool Telescope, situated on top of an extinct volcano on the Canary Island of La Palma, which is the world's largest robotic telescope. Unlike a conventional telescope, a "robotic telescope" gathers data according to computer programs written for it, and then sends it back to Liverpool for processing.

Dr Newsam led the audience through such mysteries of the night sky as recently exploded supernovae, gamma ray bursts and super massive black holes. "The Universe is a dramatic, ever-changing place but, up until recently, it has been very difficult to study these changes," said Dr Newsam. "Now, thanks to the fully robotic telescopes that the UK has built, we are at last able to start plugging this gap in our knowledge. The Cosmos has become our laboratory."

Dr Newsam went on to explain that understanding more about the Universe means understanding more about the laws of physics. "If you look at things in a new way you will learn things you didn't expect to learn," he said.

Recipe Corner Easter Egg

A 1950's recipe that's chocolate free!

EASTER has been long associated with eggs. The egg is a symbol of new life in general and of spring in particular. Christians adopted it because though an egg appears to be like the stone of a tomb, a bird hatches from it with life; which is a reminder that Jesus rose from the grave.

There has been a long tradition of giving eggs at Easter, and children in the North of England would go begging from door to door, saying "Please, Mrs Whiteleg, Please to give us an Easter egg. If you won't give us an Easter egg, Your hens will lay all coddled eggs."

Chocolate eggs only appeared in the early 19th century, coming from France and Germany, and by 1874 the Illustrated London News could remark upon their growing popularity as imports. In England, John Cadbury made the first Cadbury Easter Eggs in 1875.

Here is a 1950s egg recipe for Easter from the Wessex and Jersey Branch of the National Association of Flower Arrangement Societies:

Savoury Egg Mousse

Ingredients:
10 hard boiled eggs (8 if large)
2 tablespoon mushroom ketchup (available Waitrose)
Crushed garlic or garlic salt to taste
½ pt cream
2 tablespoons anchovy essence
4 heaped teaspoons gelatine dissolved in 1 tablespoon cold water, and one of hot.

Method:

Put yolks through a hair sieve. Whip cream stiff, add sauces, gelatine and lastly add whites of egg chopped up finely. Set in dish and decorate with chopped aspic. Served with brown bread and butter, or cold meats.

Easter Edition 2013

Portelet Protection Plan

Two fish species studied

A joint survey by a team from the Department of the Environment and Hawaii Institute of Marine Biology has been studying marine life in Portelet Bay. They've been monitoring the ballan wrasse around the reefs and the sand-dwelling rays.

Ballan wrasse grow to around 66 cm, and are female for their first eight years before a few fish change into males. The small-eyed ray is a flat-bodied fish which mostly lives on the sea floor. Both species were implanted with small transmitters and underwater receivers were used to find out how far they roam and how fast they grow.

The aim of the study was to see if Portelet would be a suitable Marine Protected Area. These are increasingly used for conservation and management of fish. Portelet Bay contains a mixture of kelp reef and sandy habitats, suitable for both wrasse and rays. Detection patterns showed that the wrasse were year round residents of the bay, while rays were occasional repeat visitors. Results suggest that ballan wrasse are good candidates for protection in Portelet, whereas this would be little benefit to rays.

Marine protected areas afford significant protection from fishing and are strikingly effective in rebuilding fish stocks. Jersey has been described as a tourist destination providing some of the finest Bass fishing to be found anywhere in Europe, and it is important that stocks are protected as well as fished for tourists and locals alike.

Power Steering

Deputy volunteers as 'shoebox' driver

BACK in December 2012, volunteer drivers Deputy Sean Power and Bob de la Haye left Jersey, taking 2,850 shoeboxes of gifts donated by Islanders to Romania. A team of students and teachers from Beaulieu Convent School (who also helped with the packing) also travelled over independently to help with distribution.

It was a memorable and difficult week. When the air brakes on the articulated trailer malfunctioned, the two drivers had an unplanned stop in Regensburg, Bavaria. After a three day delay for parts, they left Regensburg on and did a marathon 13 hour drive across Germany, Austria, Hungary and into Romania, with some atrocious driving weather.

Deputy Power said "My main motivation in coming down here has been to help drive this big truck down, but now that I've seen what they do on the ground here it sort of drives your motivation up one level to try and do a little bit more the next time."

Mustard Seed (Jersey) is a small charity set up in Jersey, Channel Isles in 1998 by Rose Hélie. Its aim is to ease suffering in eastern Europe, by providing opportunities to enable people to become self-sufficient, through the taking of humanitarian aid, funding various projects and prayerfully supporting a number of projects.

For more information, please go to www.mustardseedjersey.co.uk

Easter Edition 2013

Appeal for an eel! Help needed for slippery problem

LENT is traditionally a time for giving up, and giving to others. Part of the Parish fund raising for Christian Aid during Lent is by Lent Lunches, which take place at St Brelade's Parish Hall on Fridays between noon and 2.00 pm, and are provided by members of St Brelade's Churches, each Church acting in rotation on successive Fridays. For a modest donation, there is simple and tasty fare to enjoy - freshly made soups, bread, crackers and cheese, with tea or coffee.

The final lunch, Good Friday on April 6, 2013, always has two soups. Traditionally, one is Conger Eel, a popular Jersey dish, but this year the team have been unable to obtain a Conger Eel. If you can help, please contact the Parish Hall on 741141.

Easter Edition 2013

Parishioners invited to comment on TTS scheme

THE Minister for Transport and Technical Services (TTS) Deputy Kevin Lewis, is working in association with Constable Steve Pallett, to bring forward a scheme to improve the road, parking and public areas around St Brelade's Parish Hall, St. Aubin.

A community steering group set up and chaired by the Connétable including representatives from both the business and residential community, will oversee the final stages of the proposals.

TTS has done some initial work but is now looking for input from the local community and parishioners. They will shortly be talking individually to businesses and residents in the immediate area about the proposals to re-organise the St. Aubin village area. A planned drop-in session will then be organised at the Parish Hall, on 17 and 18 of July, for anyone who would like to meet the Parish and TTS team.

Changes to the area of St Aubin's have long been a topic of discussion. In particular, it became clear at a weekend long community gathering in 2008, 'The St. Aubin Forum', that residents and businesses were keen for improvements to be made to this vitally important and historic area of the Parish.

Now that funding has been made available for village improvements, St Aubin will be the first of a number of planned schemes that will be presented in future years. The proposed changes will offer opportunities to improve the public areas in the immediate vicinity of St Aubin including the possibility of installing an historically contextual work of art in the area in front of the Parish Hall.

Connétable Steve Pallett said: "I am extremely excited at the prospect of working with both TTS and the project team to improve the environment around St. Aubin both for those who live and work in the area and for the many visitors to the Island who are charmed by its beauty."

Summer Edition 2013

Branchage revision

Variable dates make more sense say Constables

The Comité des Connetables are proposing changes to the Loi (1914) sur la Voirie, the law which governs the Parish branchage. If passed, the following major changes will take place:

The branchage visits shall be carried out in the three-week period starting on 24th June each year and in the three-week period starting on 1st September in each year. This allows greater flexibility in timing of the Visite du Branchage now that spring growth tends to start earlier.

If there are multiple occupants of a property such as a block of flats sharing a communal area then the person liable for the foncier rate would also be liable if the branchage is not cut. This would be the co-ownership association (in the case of flying freehold); or the company (in the case of share transfer flats).

Failure to cut the branchage by the date of the Visite would incur a civil penalty, not exceeding £50. A notice would then be levied on them specifying the branches, obstacle or other deleterious matter that is to be removed and specifying that it is to be removed within a week. If they fail to do this, they would be guilty of a further offence punishable by a fine not exceeding £500.

They would be able to choose whether to have the matter dealt with summarily by the Centenier or by the Magistrate. The maximum penalty a Centenier may impose is 40% of the penalty for which the Magistrate could impose.

The Connétable could also arrange a third party to undertake the branchage work required and to recover the cost as a civil debt from the person who should have undertaken the work.

Summer Edition 2013

Accident of history

More than a car park, but a memorial park.

IN 1961, the States agreed to the purchase of "Woodford Park" on behalf of the public of the Island. But the park was not given its present name of "The Sir Winston Churchill Memorial Park" until 1966. The reason for this was one of those curious accidents of history.

The Jersey Evening Post had sponsored a memorial to the late Sir Winston Churchill, who had died in 1965 by way of a "penny fund" with members of the public contributing.

The Publics Works Committee was tasked with finding a suitable site, and suggested The Royal Square was the best place, but the States decided otherwise. Consequently, the Committee had to quickly find another suitable locale, and decided to put the memorial in Woodford Park, and rename the park accordingly.

On 5th December 1966, the Bailiff, Sir Robert Le Masurier unveiled the memorial. Also present on the chilly December morning were Lady Le Masurier, Mr Arthur Harrison of the JEP, the President of Public Works, Deputy Reg Jeune, and Mr M.B. Gulliver of L'Etacq Quarries, together with around 70 members of the general public

The bronze relief portrait of Sir Winston Churchill's head and shoulders was sculpted by Mr Anthony Gray.

The memorial stone on which it sits is made from a naturally hewn granite from L'Etacq. To keep the natural hew, only the base of the stone was worked, and also the panel for the inscription; the remained of the stone is as it was when it came out of the quarry. It is a fine monument to the great war time leader.

Summer Edition 2013

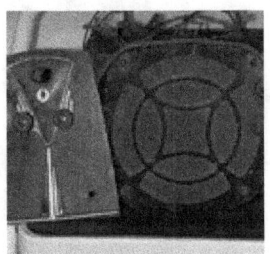

Parishioners remember: Liberation and radios

by Tony Bellows in conversation with Reg Langlois

I will never forget the day the adults started acting strangely, dancing and calling out to each other. I was playing in the back yard when my father called me indoors to listen to the wireless. "What's a wireless?" I asked. He was indoors by then so I hurried in to join the family. In all the excitement I remember there was a lot of laughing and crying and everyone was hugging each other. My father stood over by the fireplace with a strange piece of equipment in his hand that I had never seen before. It was attached to a dark coloured box-shaped thing on the floor and had wires attached to something I recognized as a battery. Sounds and voices came from it and my father told everyone to be quiet because Winston Churchill was going to speak. You could have heard a pin drop as Dad said softly "we have waited a long time for this moment".

We heard the British Prime Minister, Sir Winston Churchill, say "our dear Channel Islands are also to be freed today." There was silence in the room. It was hard to believe that the long war and the occupation of our islands were over. When I asked my father where the wireless had come from he explained that it had been in the sitting room all the time, in a cupboard under the floor next to the fireplace.

He went on to tell me that, when the Germans arrived in Jersey at the beginning of the occupation, they requisitioned his brand new Studebaker car but, before they took it away, he had very carefully removed the radio so that it did not look as if there had ever been one. If they had caught him with a radio he would have been punished or, worse still, sent to Germany.

Many detainees were sent to Germany from Jersey and never returned. They died over there. My father's car was never returned to him but I have a memento - that radio is in my loft.

Summer Edition 2013

Happy Landings

Brian raises £17,000 in charity sky-dive

LAST year Brian Clarke decided to make a sponsored sky-dive in aid of Sanctuary House, but because of inclement weather, had to postpone the event several times. But on 5th May, he was told that the jump instructors were in the Island, and the weather would be suitable.

After being instructed in operational matters, he was soon dressed in a jump suit strapped to an instructor, sitting in a small aeroplane with a big square hole in its side though which they would make the jump. At 1,000 feet they closed this door. The view from that height was spectacular, with the sea shades of translucent blue. The plane circled until it was 2 miles above the Island, and then they opened the door, and he left the plane, sitting on the instructor's lap.

This was how he described the descent: "Over we go, falling and twisting and steadying, face down, looking at the approaching Island - it is approaching rather fast, then the parachute opens and the wind noise is gone and we float. This is nice I thought, until the instructor demonstrates his skill at twirling. I plead 'that makes me really queasy', so we revert to a float as I hyperventilate, and think to myself that this raised around £17,000 and I have earned it."

As the ground approached he had to lift his legs, which was a struggle in the tight jump suit with straps binding him, so that instead of sliding on the beach, he flipped over with his face down in the sand, and his instructor on top of him! But it is a safe landing, and they both walk away.

Would he do it again? He says that "for me the moral of this story is that walking is best!"

Summer Edition 2013

Fresh Fields

Case for healthier and more sustainable food

On 15 May, the Jersey Organic Association held a showing of the film "Fresh" at Les Creux Bowling Club. It was introduced by the Chairman of the Association, Brian Adair, (pictured opposite) who explained how it highlighted the case for healthier, more sustainable food.

Made in the USA by Ana Joanes and subtitled "New thinking about what you are eating", the film is a perceptive look at what is wrong with our conventional food production system; it contrasting mass production methods with organic environmentally friendly farming.

Industrialised farming techniques involve masses of animals crammed together in unsanitary sheds, pumped full of antibiotics to prevent diseases, crops sprayed with highly toxic pesticides, and fields requiring heavy doses of fertiliser to compensate for the depleted soil. By contrast, the farmers depicted in "Fresh" have free range farm chickens, cows and pigs, and use traditional practices such as field rotation and soil enrichment with earthworms to produce fresh organic food that is healthy to eat.

While Jersey does not have the mass industrialised farming of the USA, and we can still enjoy the sight of the Jersey cow grazing in fields, cheap convenience foodstuffs often come from such sources, as the recent recall of food tainted with horse meat demonstrated.

Buying local products and organic and fair-trade products helps to boost the local economy, lessens exposure to harmful pesticides, and improves the taste and quality of your food.

Summer Edition 2013

Scouting the Heavens - Cubs entertained by Astronomy Club

Earlier this year, there were two specially arranged visits by the ACSL 6th Trinity Cub Pack to the Jersey Astronomy Club at Les Creux, with Cub Leader Katrina Rondel.

The Club Secretary, Jodie Masterman, prepared a Powerpoint presentation entitled "What is Astronomy", which took the cubs through such topics as the tools used to study celestial objects, and the moon, planets of the solar system, the sun, stars, constellations , finding the pole star and galaxies. The cubs also played a game in which they had to identify the planets from an inflatable solar system set, and holding them, stand in the right order. There was also a quiz on the differences between stars and planets, and a demonstration of a motorized solar system. A lively question and answer session followed.

During first visit, the sky was clear enough for small groups of cubs to be taken out to the dome to view Jupiter and the Moon though the telescope.

Summer Edition 2013

135

FA Cup comes to ST. Brelade

Early in June, DW Health Club & St Brelade's Bay Hotel hosted the FA Cup, and the public had a chance to come and be photographed with the famous trophy. The owner of the health club and St Brelade's Bay Hotel, Dave Whelan, is also Chairman of Wigan Athletic, and brought the cup over to Jersey. It was the first FA cup title for Wigan Athletic when they beat Manchester City 1-0 at Wembley on 11 May. Ben Watson scored the winning goal, despite missing half the season with a broken leg.

Mr Whelan said of the victory: "I am not normally nervous but I felt emotional all day. But I had a dream. I said we'd beat Everton and then Man City 1-0 in the final. It was a fantastic dream and it came true."

Summer Edition 2013

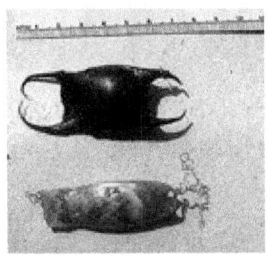

Case for shark eggs

St. Brelade's shoreline environment

When we say 'sharks eggs' we mean the black and sometimes brown (hopefully empty) 'mermaid's purses', most commonly those of lesser spotted dogfish (Scyliorhinuis canicula), a member of the shark family.

The egg cases, with embryos inside, are attached to rocks by the female dogfish, After the dogfish hatch the egg cases break free and frequently wash up onto our shoreline and beaches Dogfish around Jersey are very common and some fishermen find them a nuisance, but feeding mainly on decapod crustaceans and fishes they are good indicator of a healthy marine environment.

Their specific distribution around Jersey shores is not fully known, but as their egg cases are attached to rocks in the intertidal zone, the south east coast is likely to be the most ideal breeding ground. Spawning can take place almost all year round except mid summer although there are seasonal patterns in spawning activity thought to be equated to sea temperature.

As a bottom feeder, adult dogfish are often brought up in trawl nets, but being of little commercial value are thrown back - although larger ones are sometimes landed and may be sold as 'rock salmon'.

Summer Edition 2013

Where is summer? Its origins as a word explored

We might be asking where has summer gone, but where does the word itself come from?

Summer is the second and warmest season of the year, coming between spring and autumn seasons; reckoned astronomically from the summer solstice (21 June) to the autumnal equinox (22 or 23 September).

It is an old English word, first mentioned in 825AD in the Vespasian Psalter - "sumur & lenten", and has had various spellings - sumor, sumer, somer, sommer, symmer before taking the spelling "summer" in the 17th century.

The Jerriais word for summer is 'Êté', which is much the same as the French - 'Èté' It comes from the Old French 'esté', which in turn comes from the Latin, aestas and is related to the word for seething heat, aestus! Some hope!

Summer Edition 2013

Not a lot know that! St. Brelade place names explored

"La Moye" is a place name meaning a heap, usually stony. The name comes from the Jersey Norman French word "mouaie" and is given to promontories whose character made them resemble large heaps, whether viewed from the sea or inland.

Guernsey also has a place called La Moye for the same reason, and other Parishes in Jersey have variants of the name "" Moie, Moée, Moez.

The granite quarries of La Moye, St Brelade supplied stone for the Thames Embankment.

Summer Edition 2013

Faces of the Great War
Jersey Heritage project for exhibition

NEXT year will be the 100th anniversary of the start of the First World War. Locally, Jersey Heritage is planning to mark it in several ways, one of which is a project called "Faces of the Great War". The purpose of the project is to collect copies of images of Islanders who played a part in the war as servicemen or civilians, mount an exhibition and create a visual memorial of the Great War.

In 1919 the States of Jersey created a Roll of Service; the Great War Study Group are working on a revised and updated version of this. Jersey Heritage proposes to put a face to the names.

Between April and July 2013, Jersey Heritage will hold collecting days in each of the twelve parishes. We are inviting parishioners to bring along their photographs, letters and objects relating to the Great War to be recorded, scanned and photographed while they wait. They also want any information about the part played by the Island's overlooked French community.

There will be a short talk about the project on Monday 15 July at St Brelade's Parish Hall from 2.00 pm to 3.30 pm after which curator Chris Addy, Julia Coutanche and colleagues from Jersey Archive will be on hand to take notes, scan images and talk to people about their material.

As well as the special collecting days in the parishes, Jersey Heritage will also be holding other collecting days at the Jersey Archive and Jersey Museum throughout the year.

For more information, please contact Julia Coutanche at the Jersey Museum on telephone 633342 or email julia.coutanche@jerseyheritage.org

Summer Edition 2013

g

Noirmont Liberation Service

First Liberation Day service at Noirmont

LIBERATION Day this year saw the very first St Brelade's Parish Liberation Day Service held at Noirmont Point. Constable Steve Pallett worked with in conjunction with the Channel Islands Occupation Society and former Deputy Bob Hill.

A letter in the JEP on 22nd August 1945 suggested that Noirmont headland should be purchased for the people of Jersey. Prior to the war, the headland was privately owned and off limits to the public. This letter led to a lengthy debate in the States, ending on 22nd January 1947, when they finally agreed to purchase the headland on condition it be retained as a War Memorial to all those Islanders who lost their lives during WWII - some 450 men, women and children. The price of the headland was £9,000 of which £1,187 and 16 shillings was made up of public subscriptions.

The Memorial Stone that we see today was placed by the Public Works Dept. on 9th May, 1970 to commemorate the 25th anniversary of Liberation, at a cost of £25.

A simple service was led by the Rector, the Reverend Mark Bond, after which four wreaths were laid at the base of the memorial by Constable Steve Pallett, Chief Minister Ian Gorst, the President of the Channel Islands Occupation Society, Paul Burnal, and Bob Hill on behalf of the Jersey Human Rights Group.

St.Aubin plans unveiled

Final proposals hoped for late autumn.

A consultation by Transport and Technical Services on St Aubin regarding calming and public realm improvements took place at the Parish Hall in July. Two options were presented as a basis for discussion "" Option A "Improving the Village Centre", and Option B "Improving the Car park and Promenade".

There was also a questionnaire available for completion. 250 people were estimated to have attended the two days of consultation, and 109 questionnaires were completed. Of those replying, 55% lived in the Village, 29% from other parts of St Brelade, and remaining 16% came from other parishes.

The general consensus, both from questionnaire and discussions was firmly against creating additional car parking spaces by removing some of the green space ("Option B") that green zone between La Neuve Route and the sea wall was considered very important by residents. There was no objection to losing the shelter, though some covered benches were favoured. But there was general agreement that the existing car park layout was poor, and could be improved to ensure smoother flow of traffic without any loss of spaces. There was a desire to see conflicts resolved between pedestrians, cyclists and vehicles.

Some residents wished for parking permits, but very few respondents supported proposals to change disc parking to short stay car parking. Traffic calming measures were generally supported. There were mixed opinions over the proposed loss of the central traffic island. If to be removed, people considered there should be more crossing points.

Finalised proposals will now be drawn up in consultation between TTS and the St. Aubin Project Board, and these will be presented at a further drop-in session planned for early October. It is envisaged that work on planned changes would begin early next year and hoped to be completed by Easter.

Autumn Edition 2013

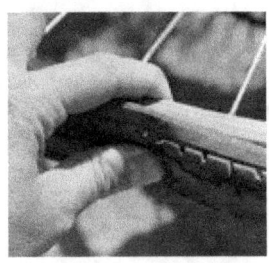

Cyclists want culprit nailed!

Railway Walk tacks puncture bike tyres

IDIOTIC vandals who scattered razor-sharp tacks along the Railway Walk in St Brelade are putting cyclists, children, runners and dogs in serious danger, says the manager of a cycle hire business. He called the police after receiving desperate calls from people stranded with punctures from St Aubin to Corbiére over the August Bank Holiday weekend.

The tacks, which are like tiny nails, have also caused misery for parents who have been left with punctured pushchair wheels. Their appearance follows the placing of a sign on a tree on the Railway Walk saying, "This is a cycle track not a race track". It is not clear whether the two are linked and someone has a vendetta against cyclists.

Steve Booth, of Zebra Cycle, is reported as saying that he 'had not seen anything like it in 30 years in the cycle hire business'. "It is 100 per cent stupid and idiotic," he said. "I was getting a lot of phone calls from that side of the Island over the weekend."

St. Brelade Honorary Police told La Baguette: "If anyone has information that could lead us to identify the person or persons responsible, please contact the Duty Centenier on 741175 or Crimestoppers on 0800 555 111 if you would prefer to remain anonymous."

Autumn Edition 2013

Putting the clock back

Autumn is the time for getting an extra hour!

The word 'autumn' comes from the Old French autompn (around the 13th century), and took its modern spelling in the 17th century.

Before that people just called the season 'Harvest'. Jérriais, however, has no word for the season, and makes do with September - "this Autumn" is "ches S'tembre". One of earliest uses of Autumn is Tyndale's Bible (1526) - "Trees rotten in authum."(Jude 8).

Autumn is the third season of the year, reckoned astronomically from the descending equinox to the winter solstice; from 21 September to 21 December in the Northern hemisphere, athough popularly it comprises the months September, October, and November.

The term "œFall"☐ for the season comes from Old English - "to fall or to die", referring to falling leaves. It was supplanted in England during the 18th century, but retained in America - "Spring tyme, Somer, faule of the leafe, and winter". It is a useful term for remembering to change clocks "" "Sping forward, Fall back"

A famous literary reference is John Keats' poem, To Autumn, 1820:

Season of mists and mellow fruitfulness,
Close bosom-friend of the maturing sun;
Conspiring with him how to load and bless
With fruit the vines that round the thatch-eves run;
To bend with apples the moss'd cottage-trees,
And fill all fruit with ripeness to the core

Clocks go forward 1 hour on Sunday 27th October

Autumn Edition 2013

Put on the spot

Search is on find an appropriate sculpture for Parish Hall

Alongside schemes proposed by Transport and Technical Services for the regeneration of St Aubin, there has also been a parallel consultation looking at improving the semi-circular area in front of the Parish Hall. Chris Clifford, a Public Art Consultant liaising with Planning Department has been tasked by ConnÃ©table Steve Pallett regarding financing and ideas for a public piece of art for the front of the Parish Hall.

Mr Clifford told La Baguette that it was likely that some funding could be obtained under the "percentage for art" planning policy, and two potential developments in St Brelade had been identified where the developers may be agreeable to their percentage being used for this purpose. He is confident that more will be forthcoming in months ahead, and a scheme to raise additional capital by public subscription may also be a possibility.

About 35 people gave written responses to the questionnaire, and Mr Clifford also spoke to around 20 people during the two day consultation at the Parish Hall.

A common theme was that the area should be decluttered, with unnecessary and obtrusive signage removed. Several options were on display including one design of a boat-shaped granite sculpture with a place for floral arrangements.

A spiral maze design proved popular, and also on the agenda was a sculpture of a notable figure with connections to the Parish, such as the Royalist Privateer Sir George Carteret, or St Aubin of Angers himself.

The next step will be a public meeting to report the findings of the consultation, and gaining consensus from Parishioners on which design they want. It is hoped that this initiative will follow on from the proposed St. Aubin improvements.

Autumn Edition 2013

Bin on the beach

With 'a good dose of seaside humour'

There are new recycling bins on Jersey beaches, aiming to encourage locals and tourists to dispose of beach rubbish in a sustainable manner. The first phase of the project sees recycling points at eight beach locations, four of which are in St Brelade - Ouaisne car park; Wayside, St Brelade's Bay; St Brelade's Bay promenade and La Braye slip. More locations will follow if the scheme is a success.

Recycling Manager for TTS, Emma Richardson, said "Beach-goers now have the opportunity to recycle their cans, plastic bottles and glass before they go home." Colourful signage to complement the bins has been designed by local artist Edward Blampied. It is a lively cartoon with "a good dose of seaside humour".

Islanders are reminded that the new beach recycling banks should not be used for general household recycling. These new facilities are much smaller than the Island-wide recycling 'bring banks' and have been designed only to receive the recyclables generated by beach-goers.

Autumn Edition 2013

Post-it notes

Jersey Post is keeping its mouth shut

Jersey Post have undertaken a detailed statistical review of post boxes. As a result, they will be closing 25% of the post boxes with very little usage. Other changes involve moving collection times for 35 boxes to earlier in the day. At the same time, collection services from sub-post offices will be significantly increased.

Post boxes effected by the closure in St Brelade are Ouaisne, Corbiere, St Aubin's High Street, Ravencliffe, La Pulente, Mont Fondan. Other boxes which may be relocated are Elizabeth Avenue (to Spar) and St Brelade's Bay (to a more central location). On closure, boxes will be sealed and plates put in advising of the nearest alternative box.

Andy Jehan, director of postal operations said "We used to employ extra staff around the summer holiday period to deal with the extra volume of postcards, but now tourists are more likely to use electronic means of communication". Chief Executive Kevin Keen has spoken to La Baguette, emphasising that they are aware of the historical importance of the post box, first introduced to Jersey and Guernsey by Anthony Trollope as a pilot scheme before being rolled out across the UK. They are liaising with Jersey Heritage and Planning regarding listing of historical boxes, like the Victorian one in St Aubin's High Street, and that no precipitate action will be taken regarding removing boxes.

Autumn Edition 2013

Parishioners remember

Former St. Brelade Deputy and Constable Enid Quenault

Born in Trinity to a farming family, Enid Quenault moved to St Ouen when she was two. In those days, St Ouen was a very small farming community, and her father, Arthur Quérée grew crops and flowers.

She stayed there until 1953, when she moved with her husband to St Brelade, and her present home on Rue du Conet. "It wasn't a tarmac road in those days," she recalls, "only a rough track with grass growing in the middle".

She first attended the Girls Collegiate School in Colomberie, but there were no buses when the Germans occupied Jersey, so she stayed in St Ouen and attended the Parish School.

As children, she and her brother used to go down to the sea wall being built by Russian slave workers, and scavenge for firewood, which they collected in an old pram. They also used cut-up car tyres for their bicycles; "It was make do and mend." Enid recalls.

She attended the States Intermediate School (which became Hautlieu) alongside Iris Le Feuvre, Bill Morvan and John Farley, all future States members like herself. She had planned to be a teacher, but took a job at the Midland Bank when that came up. Approached by Constable John Chévalier, she stood and was elected as Deputy in 1975 to the newly created St Brelade Number 2 district, where an extra seat had just been added, and later became Constable of the Parish from 1987 to 1999.

On her 24 years in office, she recalls "I was so well supported by my husband, Ernest." She has two children, one of whom, Deputy Ann Pryke, has followed her mother's footsteps into the States.

Mrs Quénault enjoyed her time in the States. One of her notable memories is when she was President of the Broadcasting Committee. The States had finally decided that the BBC would provide a local radio service, and she recalls travelling to Broadcasting House to sign a special charter for the BBC to commence operations in Jersey.

As well as politics, she followed her father, former St Ouen Deputy Arthur Quérée in being a Methodist lay preacher, and in 2010, she celebrated 50 years of lay preaching.

In a way, she reflected, she had achieved her ambition of being a teacher, after all.

Autumn Edition 2013

Kids club hammers ahead

New after-school activity scheme for 6-12 year olds

The 'Woodpeckers Fun Club' is a new venture for school children ages 6 to 12 at the St Brelade Youth Club Project, Communicare. It provides after school facilities from 3pm to 6pm.

Mrs Heloisa Le Gresley, founder of the club, said the idea for the club came when she noticed mothers struggling to juggle school and work commitments. Currently with a qualified staff of four, the club can accommodate 40 children. Transport of children to the club is available. The club provides healthy snacks, craft work, an indoor play area, games, and outings in fine weather to the playing fields and Elephant Park.

For more information, please contact Heloisa Le Gresley 07797749962 or email: woodpeckersfunclub@gmail.com

Autumn Edition 2013

Creepy House Reading challenge for children

The Annual Summer Reading Challenge at Quennevais Library saw the construction of a "Creepy House" to encourage children to take part. The challenge takes place at libraries all across the UK. It is designed for children aged four to eleven, who have to read six books. These are read in stages, with two books each stage.

At the end of each stage, the child will come back to the library to tell the library staff about the stories, while sitting inside the "Creepy House". They will receive stickers on the way, and some are designed to release a stink when scratched. There are also special codes to unlock fun on the Summer Challenge website, and once the challenge is complete, the child gets a glow in the dark wrist band. During the next school term, there will also be certificates handed out at school assemblies.

Les Quennevais usually sees around 300 children taking part, of which around 250 complete the challenge. It is a good way for children to visit the library at an early age, encouraging a love of books, and helping children develop language and literacy.

Autumn Edition 2013

New headteachers for schools

John Baudains (36) has been acting head of Mont Nicholle school since November and is now confirmed as permanent head teacher following the early retirement of Colin Masterman due to ill health.

John was previously assistant head at Grouville School, where he had worked since 2003. He began his career at the school he now leads. "Mont Nicolle is where I started teaching and I am delighted to be taking the school forward on the next part of its learning journey. I have really enjoyed the past two terms and it is a real pleasure to be given the opportunity to lead the team. I am looking forward to working with the whole school community," Mr Baudains said.

Sarah Hague, the former deputy head of Les Quennevais school takes over as head teacher at the start of the autumn term. Mrs Hague (41) has worked at the school for 14 years and teaches GCSE law and religious studies. She succeeds John Thorp, who retired earlier this year .

"I feel it is an immense privilege to be given the opportunity to lead such an exceptional school. Les Quennevais School is a very special place and, having been part of it for 14 years"☐ She said "I am extremely excited about the future of the school and I look forward to building on the success it has achieved under the dedicated guidance of John Thorp," said Mrs Hague.

Julian Bernstein, the Chair of Les Quennevais Board of Governors, said: "After a rigorous selection process, Sarah Hague won through against both national and local competition."

"We are very pleased to be able to make this appointment and I think it's a testament to Mrs Hague's professionalism that she was able to excel against such a strong field. We look forward to a positive future for Les Quennevais under her leadership."

La Baguette extend their best wishes to John and Sarah - and look foward to reporting on both schools activities in forthcoming editions.

Autumn Edition 2013

Blanket Appeal

When there's a wool, there's a way

Every Wednesday morning, the Friendship Group meet at Communicare to knit squares that are stitched into blankets for poor and needy families in Romania. They are are collected by Rosemary Coote MBE of the Friends of Ecco Homo Trust.

The last appeal in La Baguette was in early 2012, and their supply of knitting wool is now running low. Amy Mathys of the Friendship Group is appealing for anyone with spare wool to donate it to this worthy cause. Double-ply is mostly used but anything will be used and very much appreciated. The wool can be dropped off at Communicare, or Amy will arrange collection. Her telephone number is 745772.

Autumn Edition 2013

Bang goes the theory!

Graduate guest speaker at Astronomy Club

THE Astronomy Club listened to a presentation by Tom Hathaway, M.Phys (Lancs) a parish resident and former Les Quennevais student, on the topic - "Any Suitably Advanced Cosmology Is Indistinguishable From Magic".

The story began with ancient Greek pioneers "" Parmenides, Anaxagoras, Epicurus, and Philolaus, ending with the fixed geocentric model in Ptolomy's Almagest. But with Copernicus, Galileo, Kepler and Newton, that was overturned by the model of planets revolving in elliptical orbits around the sun.

Mr Hathaway talked about advent of modern astronomers such as Slipher, Wirtz, Willem de Sitter, Hubble (after whom the space telescope was named) and Eddington. Eddington sent out a team to photograph an eclipse, proving Einstein's theory of relativity, which predicted that light would be bent by the gravity of the sun, so that stars hidden behind it would be visible. The 20th century saw the conflict between the supporters of a "steady state" universe which existed forever, and the "Big Bang" with the creation of the universe at a fixed time in the past. Mr Hathaway concluded with modern problems such as Dark Matter and Dark Energy.

In questions afterwards, Mr Hathaway explained different methods for locating extra-solar planets, which cannot actually be seen. Members expressed thanks to Mr Hathaway for a fascinating talk, and hoped he would return for another.

Puppy Walking Happy at home with Jacqui

"Happy" is a Guide dog puppy residing at the St. Brelade home of Jacqui Richomme and her husband Dick. "Happy" arrived in August 2012 aged 8 weeks will be on the island until about 12 to 14 months old.

As a Puppy Walker, Jacqui gives "Happy" basic training and socialising in readiness for her professional training in London. "It is important that the puppy experiences as many different environments as possible in order to prepare her for what she is likely to encounter in her working life, leaning to be relaxed around a variety of different sounds and smells" she told La Baguette.

In her smart blue "Guide Dog Puppy in Training" jacket, "Happy" has visited many local restaurants, pubs, cafes, shops and supermarkets where she has been made very welcome. It can be very hard to resist fussing a pup but people are starting to understand that when they see a Guide Dog Pup working that it is to be treated in the same way as a qualified working dog and that it is important to ignore her and let her concentrate on her trainer and commands she is being given.

"Happy" has visited St Lawrence Primary School to meet children doing a project on Guide Dogs. This has been a good opportunity to explain what the puppies are being taught and what they will achieve.

This is a pilot scheme that The Guide Dog Association is currently running in Jersey. At this stage of the pup's life the Guide Dog Association covers the cost of dietary requirements and veterinary care.

Mandy, the Puppy Walker Supervisor comes to the island every 5 or 6 weeks to check on the pup's progress and to provide support and guidance. They are looking to interview suitable puppy walkers in September anyone interesting can email Jacqui at j.richomme@hotmail.com.

Autumn Edition 2013

Greatest Coffee morning

Cancer charity aim to cause a bit of a stir

THE 'Macmillan Jersey Cancer Support's Greatest Coffee Morning' will see many coffee mornings held throughout the island starting in September and St Brelade held one at St Brelade's Parish Hall on Friday 27th September. "Coffee, tea, cakes, and even bacon butties " were available, says Kandidprint's Ian Le Sueur, who supported the event in memory of his mother, who sadly passed away earlier in the month.

The event originated in 2011 as a scheme to raise awareness of Macmillan Jersey's work and fast became a popular fundraising event. All proceeds from the coffee mornings go towards ensuring high quality and comprehensive services are available to people affected by cancer in Jersey.

Macmillan Cancer Support (Jersey) offers information, support and practical advice to anyone affected by cancer. The service is free and confidential and available to patients, their families, friends and carers, as well as health care professionals.

For more information, see www.macmillanjersey.com.

Autumn Edition 2013

Not a lot of people know that

Where does the name 'Ouaisne' come from?

Ouaisné (pronounced "Way Nay") is the name given to the bay to the east of St Brelade's Bay.

According to Dr Frank Le Maistre, the word means an anchorage, perhaps because the bay was sheltered by the La Cotte headland affording a safe anchorage for small ships.

Early forms of the name are Hoisnet, Hoinet (in a map of 1810), and Houéné (in a map of 1844).

Stone was taken by boat from the quarries at Ouaisné in the 18th century for the building of St Aubin's Chapel.

Ouaisne Common is one of the Island's richest and most diverse nature reserves and designated a Site of Special Interest (SSI).

Autumn Edition 2013

Stuffed Apples

Make the most of an autumn crop

TRADITIONALLY autumn is the time for apples to ripen and fall. The taste of apples immediately evokes the bright colours of the changing leaves, and the crisp cool air of the season. Apples are remarkably versatile and most people have a favourite recipe, often handed down through the family. But here's a good-looking and tasty starter to make use of that autumn crop of apples.

Ingredients:
6 fair sized Cox's Orange Pippin apples
1 oz. walnuts (reserve 1½ for garnish and chop the rest)
A little watercress and/or lettuce for garnish.
8 oz. carton cottage cheese with pineapple
4 oz. peeled prawns (or small tin of peeled shrimps)

(i>Method:
Cut the top off each apple then, using a teaspoon, scoop out the centre to within a quarter of an inch of the skin.
Discard the cores but chop the flesh finely and put into a mixing-bowl and stir into it all the other ingredients - except the garnishings.
Rub cut surfaces of the apples with lemon juice as you go, to keep the flesh white.
Pile the filling into the empty apple-shells, top each with a walnut quarter and a shrimp and serve on a bed of lettuce or watercress.

Autumn Edition 2013

Postal Blues

Ode to our beloved postboxes

POSTAL BLUES

Along the old post box, a snail crawls
Red metal covered with a coat of grime
The moss creeping over nearby walls
No one has been here for a long time.

Once it was a busy path, workers walked
Down to the harbour; once a thriving port
Rich merchants haggled prices, talked
Privateers bargained hard at the Old Court

But that was years ago, now all remains
Is the view, right at the top of the hill
Gone are the walkers by, gone the trains
Victoria Regina say the letters still

It is sad when fragments of the past are left
Almost a time to mourn, to feel bereft

Autumn Edition 2013

Ordinand in Training

'I look forward to the day I can return says Jo

Parishioner Jo Mulliner is "ordinand in training" at St Brelade's Church and St Aubin on the Hill. She is studying in term time at Ridely Hall, Cambridge. Half way through her course, she will soon be ordained as a priest in the Church of England.

She told La Baguette: "The last academic year has been a whirlwind of sprinting between lectures, learning New Testament Greek and exploring biblical and theological studies to a level which made my brain hurt. It is only now in the time of reflection that I can see so much of what I have processed, learnt and developed. Coupled with this has been weekly church attachment at a wonderful village church to the south of Cambridge. It therefore feels that almost every second has been filled with activity and learning."

After the summer term ended, before returning to Jersey, she was invited to help as a guest of two Parishes on the Isle of Man, and says that "It was a great experience, and good to be part of an island diocese. The photo says it all!"

Although she will need to gain Parish experience in England first, she hopes to come back to Jersey, and says "I look forward to the day when I can return to serve the people of this wonderful island who have so faithfully supported me through the ups and downs of life, and continue to do so, daily."

Autumn Edition 2013

Kevin Spacey festival feature

St Brelade Spirituality Festival

THE St Brelade's Festival of Christian Spirituality was held between 18th and 22nd of September at the Parish Church, Church Hall, St Aubin on the Hill Church and Communicare.

Alongside local guest speakers were talks by Ray Simpson, of the International Community of Aidan and Hilda, best known for his writings on "Celtic Christianity".

As well as times for prayer and worship, there were also a film screening of "Pay it Forward" starring Kevin Spacey, poetry readings by award winning poet Matt Harvey, a choral concert by the Amity Singers, and a performance of the Comedy Sci-Fi Play "The God Particle", fresh from the Edinburgh Fringe.

Co-ordinator Brian Clarke said "mind, spirit, soul and body interests were often seen as an alternative to Christianity but this Festival showed that this is not always the case."

Autumn Edition 2013

Christmas Fun

St. Brelade can be perplexing for Santa

Father Christmas sat down with a sigh. It was time to get out the maps, and refresh his memory of all the quirky little places that were difficult to find. And nowhere was more difficult that finding his way around the Island of Jersey - and particulary St. Brelade.

There were little narrow lanes which you could, if feeling adventurous, head up around 30 mph. There were one way streets which sent his poor head into a spin, and seemingly endless road works and diversions. And there were place names that had little to do with the places. After all, he thought, shouldn't Beauport Estate at least be within sight of Beauport and not halfway across the Parish?

And there were so many new buildings going up all over the place, and in recent years, Dasher was nearly dashed on that very tall Air Traffic Control Tower, as the sleigh came in to land on the La Quennevais Playing Fields - but at least the lighthouse was still standing in the right place and St Aubin should once again be ablaze with Christmas lights - a useful landmark.

Sometimes the labels on the presents had not been well written. Were they people or places? Who was Monty Le Brun? Or Clodah Roncier? Or Don Farm? And where did Rudy Genets live? And where were the Red Houses? There were plenty of houses, but none of them red. And how exactly how to pronounce Ouaisne should he need directions? And as for Ruelle a Rouaux ...eek! He scratched his head once more.

Fortunately, one of the elves was a former Roads Inspector and could guide him through the narrow lanes, the sudden changes in speed limits, the diversion sides, so that he could deliver all the presents just in time. And he could nibble at the strange foods that people put out for him to eat on his festive journey. Black Butter, which wasn't butter at all. Jersey Wonders, which seemed rather like a deep fried scone and 'bean-crock' which at least would assist in a swift return to Lapland. Would there be beer at Corbiere, he mused, as he buttoned up his red coat, and set off.

Christmas Edition 2013

First Class idea

Jersey Post 'Call and Check' scheme to be trialled in St. Brelade

JERSEY Post has begun a pilot scheme called "Call & Check" in St Brelade. Postal workers visit many homes in the island on weekdays, and are well placed to do a little more when delivering mail. Joe Dickinson, special projects officer, said Jersey Post was funding the trial to see how well it worked. "The service is independent from the post in the sense that even if there was no post for that house that day and they're on the call and check service they would still get checked on," he explained. "What we're tried to do with the pilot is to have clients from each of certain groups, so we have some people from the blind society, some people from Communicare... we tried to get a cross section as they may have slightly different needs."

The idea is that a nominated postal workers will call on people in the community on a regular basis, which might be daily, weekly or as agreed. The postie will knock on their door and have a brief chat to ask how they are and whether they have any immediate issues or requests. If they do, the information will be passed on to the appropriate organisation for action, such as their doctor or the Parish. As Joe Dickinson says "We are in no way proposing postal workers should become health carers or provide medical assistance. We just want to be a regular friendly face that frequently checks on certain individuals and can raise concerns if necessary."

The scheme is aimed at helping vulnerable people who may need assistance, such as those living alone, socially isolated and lonely, recently bereaved, carers, those isolated from the immediate community, due to physical disability or health problems, anyone who is recently out of hospital and anyone who has been assessed as benefiting from the service.

Application can be made by completing the form: please click here

For more information and further details on how referrals can be made, please contact: Joe Dickinson, Jersey Post, Rue des Pres, Jersey, JE1 1AA. Alternatively you can call Joe on (01534) 616594 or email him at call&check@jerseypost.com

Autumn Edition 2013

Not a lot of people know that!

The cold facts about winter
by Michael Le Quesne

Winter is the fourth and coldest season of the year, reckoned astronomically from the winter solstice to the vernal equinox (22 December to 20 March), but commonly used for months of December, January and February.

"Winter" came into English around 888 AD. from Germanic roots, meaning the "time of water", referring to the rain and snow which is prevalent during this season. As Shakespeare says in "As You Like it" - "As the winter to foul weather".

The winter solstice is around December 21 or 22, the shortest day of the year in the Northern hemisphere. It is from the Latin "sol" (sun) and "sistere" (to stand still) and was first used in English around 1250.

"Yule" comes from the Old Norse "jol" which referred to a heathen feast lasting 12 days, and later this mutated into the 12 days of Christmas.

Robbie Burns, in 1796, says that "Dawin it is dreary, When birks are bare at Yule", and Tennyson speaks of the bells calling people to church at Christmas: "They bring me sorrow touch'd with joy, The merry merry bells of Yule."

The Jerriais word for "winter" is "Hivé", which probably comes from the Latin hibernalis which means "wintry". The term hibernal is often used for animals which sleep or hibernate during the winter months. Perhaps Jersey folk also wanted to stay sleeping snug beside the fireside.

Stamp of approval

Special issue stamps feature Parish resident Nigel Mansell CBE

On 15 October 2013, six stamps and a souvenir sheet were issued by Jersey Post commemorating the 20th anniversary of Nigel Mansell CBE being the only driver to to simultaneously hold the Formula One and The IndyCar World Championships.

The issue, entitled Nigel Mansell - Legacy of a Formula One Champion, includes stamps which depict key moments in the St Brelade resident's illustrious motor racing career, en-route to becoming the most successful British Formula One driver of all time.

Jersey Post will donate a percentage of the first year's Philatelic sales of the issue to help secure the future of St Brelade's Youth Club, a local initiative supported by Nigel Mansell.

The Club offers activities such as 5-a-side football, pool, cooking and table tennis as well as activities and projects around the Parish.

Gary Carroll, Business Development Director at Jersey Post said "We are delighted through this issue to be able to help Nigel Mansell in his continued support and investment into the future of young people locally".

The stamps were created with the help of Nigel Mansell himself, who commented "I am tremendously excited about the launch of these new stamps, another great piece of history being documented".

"Nigel Mansell's career was high in drama, featuring a heady blend of skill and tenacity, and these graphically striking stamps capture some of its key landmarks," commented Chris Elligott, Philatelic Product Manager at Jersey Post.

Christmas Edition 2013

Exchange of ideas

Unique building 'discovered' in Parish

LA Baguette went to visit Simon Hector, of 'Ultimate Audio' at his business address - a German bunker, built to function as a telephone exchange during the Occupation.

The image of a business run inside a German bunker probably conjures up cold grey concrete walls and floors, draughts and dim lighting. But nothing could be further from the reality.

The bunker is one of three identical constructions all having being built by the Organisation Todt prior to 1st July 1943. It has walls and ceilings two metres thick, and the whole structure consisted of 850 cubic metres of reinforced concrete and would have taken approximately 3 months to complete. It is estimated it was manned by 10 -12 men with nine bunks in the main room used as the cinema room now. A small room apart provided living space for the commandant.

Simon moved to St Brelade around 4 years ago from St Helier, and at that time, the bunker beneath his house functioned as a general warehouse for another company. When their lease expired in April 2012, he saw the potential of the site for his own Hi-Fi and Home Cinema business, as it was bone dry and soundproof.

Over the next nine months, Simon, helped by by Richard Le Plongeon of the Occupation Society, worked to make it habitable, keeping the best features of the original design - such as wooden clad walls "" together with modern accessories in keeping with the style of the building. The wooden clad walls are in the 'liaisons' room where they sat on the telephone lines. He managed to source some original German artefacts, such as the heavy steel door, as well as the tasteful use of vintage bulkhead lights and bakelite light switches.

With his love of sound, Simon also has an old valve record player radiogram, which surprisingly can pick up radio signals where modern equipment cannot. In the room where the Commandant would have slept, he also has a wind up gramophone player and a collection of old 78 rpm records, such as Marlene Dietrich singing Lili Marlene.

The end result is a fusion of old and new in harmony. It is respectful of the buildings history, but functional as well as a modern sound studio.

Christmas Edition 2013

Parishioners Remember

Peter Turley recounts more memories of his time as an Avro Lancaster Rear Gunner.

PETER Turley, who is now resident at Maison St Brelade, was a young man of 21 when he was rear gunner on a Lancaster on those flights. He made 34 operational flights over Germany, and bailed out once over Belgium. One flight he remembers in particular from 1944, after the Normandy landings.

"The Lancaster was flying back home after an electrical storm knocked out one of the four engines. Another engine failed, and the aeroplane was losing height badly. The Skipper thought that it probably would not have enough power to get bank to England, so near the Belgian border, he told 5 of the crew to leave by parachute in case he had to ditch in the sea. The Skipper and the navigator struggled on with the plane, and one of the engines regained power, so they managed to limp back to Kent after all."

Meanwhile Peter Turley landed alongside a fellow crew member in the dark, in what he described as 'the muddiest field in Belgium', losing a boot on the way down.

They had no idea where the rest of the crew had landed, or whether they were behind Allied or German lines. Swiftly they stashed their parachutes out of sight in a hedgerow, and set off to find habitation, and hopefully a friendly face.

At the first house, the Flemish did not understand English, and others would not open doors, but eventually, they found a house where they were given shelter and welcome. They were given food, had a much needed wash and a good nights sleep. The following day, young men from a resistance group, wearing grey and white berets, came to the house, asked them questions in English. Once satisfied that their story was genuine, they took them to another house, to be reunited with flight engineer Nobby.

Fortunately, they were behind Allied lines not German ones. So they were taken to an RAF unit who took them to an airfield just outside Brussels, then onward to England. All the crew that jumped had made it back, unscratched apart from the odd graze and bruise, back to their squadron.

Peter still remembers the debriefing, when the chief concern of the officer concerned was the loss of the very expensive parachutes. Could they tell him where they were? Obviously, they had no idea, part from the fact that it was in a hedge bordering a field in Belgium, and it was very muddy. And for all Peter knows, they may still be there!

Christmas Edition 2013

Male Drop

Jersey Post donate letterbox to mens sanctuary charity

Jersey Post have given the recently closed post box in St Aubin's village to Caring Hands, and it will now be redeployed as a collection box. A description of the charity has replaced the box's collection time sign. The keys for the box (which is outside Murrays) were handed to Constable Steve Pallett at a ceremony on the 24th October. The Rector of St Brelade's Parish Church, Mark Bond, blessed the box and offered prayers for this outreach into the Community.

Colin Taylor, the founder of Caring Hands, said he hoped other decommissioned postboxes in the Island could be used in a similar way. He said if anyone did post an item by mistake the charity would pass it on to Jersey Post.

Collections will go to support the Men's refuge, but also for three months of the year, monies collected will also be donated to other Parish charities. The Royal British Legion will be the first to receive donations, in aid of their November Poppy Appeal.

Christmas Edition 2013

The night sky gets messier!

Astronomy Club explores deep space

The Jersey Astronomy club met in September for a talk on Messier Objects given by Jodie Masterman. The French astronomer Charles Messier was a comet hunter. In 1771, frustrated by objects which resembled comets, but which were not, he compiled a list to avoid wasting time on them. The final list came to 103 objects, but these were supplemented by other astronomers. In particular the New General Catalogue of Nebula or Clusters of Stars (NGC) was compiled by John Louis Emil Dreyer in 1888 and contains 7,840 objects.

These Messier Objects comprise five different types of deep space object - diffuse nebulae, planetary nebulae, open clusters, globular clusters and galaxies. Some are named by appearance, with names such as the Crab Nebula, the Wild Duck Cluster, the Eagle Nebular, Pillars of Creation, Swan Nebula. Others are named after figures in Greek mythology - Andromeda Galaxy, Orion Nebula, Pleiades Star Cluster.

Since they could be observed with a relatively small power telescope, they are among the brightest and therefore most visible astronomical objects (popularly called "deep sky objects"). One of the most visible objects with the naked eye is M31, which is the Great Nebula in Andromeda. This was a fascinating talk, with detailed photos of the deep sky objects to illustrate it.

Christmas Edition 2013

Special Garden Grotto

Reg reveals Santa's present plan

Father Christmas will be visiting Reg's Garden at Badgers Holt, Route des Genets, several times in the run up to Christmas. On Sundays, starting on the 17th November until the 15th December, and on two Thursdays, the 12th and 19th December, from 3.30 to 4.30, he can be found in his own special grotto. This is in the 'Class Room' a little building situated on the right, just inside the gateway as you enter the garden.

It will cost £2 for children from 3 to 8 years old and £3 for children from 8 to 10 to meet Father Christmas, and the boys and girls will be able choose a present from a lucky dip according to their age (provided they have been good!). Reg's Elves have already been at work packing presents, some of which have been donated by local shops.

The children visiting Father Christmas will have to be accompanied by an adult at all times. The event will raise money for charity, and the Father Christmas of the day will nominate the charity of their choice.

Christmas Edition 2013

Review of the Year

A look back at key events in 2013

January saw the Daniel Entwistle sculpture of Mammoth on display in the gardens of St Brelade's Bay Hotel, inspired by Jersey's pre-historic past at La Cotte just across the bay.

February, St Brelade's Bay was voted amongst the top 20 in the British Isles in Trip Advisor. And the newly Refurbished Harbour Gallery was opened by Professor Ed Sallis OBE.

March. There was severe weather with heavy snow and blizzards with a number of fallen trees. Local residents Mr and Mrs Budworth were trapped under fallen trees on railway walk before being rescued. They suffered spinal injuries, but fortunately now on the road to recovery.

A referendum on electoral reform was held on Jersey on 24 April 2013, but sadly proved to be inconclusive. Perhaps it should have been held on 1st April!

May saw the First Liberation Day Service being at Noirmont Headland, which was bought by the States as a memorial to the people of Jersey who died during the Occupation.

Nigel Mansell launched a Tree of Life project to support St Brelade's Youth Project.

Meanwhile local talent entertained with "The Reg Factor"

It was the end of an era as Les Quennevais head teacher John Thorp and Mont Nichole head Colin Masterman both retired

In the same month, St Brelade and its French twin town Granville were crowned the winners of the Jeux Inter-Jumelage - or Parish Twinning Games.

July. Sir John McColl was joined by his wife for a tour of Sanctuary House, St Aubin. He heard of how the men at the refuge had been helped and were put on the road to recovery. His Excellency said "They reached out a hand and from the community here they've been given tremendous support."

July also saw the official opening of Reg's Wildlife Garden by Mike Stentiford MBE, just before the annual "Reg Stock" festival of music.

August "Battle of Flowers" success with a Thai Elephant theme from St Brelade called Chang saw the Parish win the Prix d'Excellence and three other top awards including 'First in Class', 'Best Costumed' and 'Best Set Piece'.

September saw the St Brelade "Festival of Spirituality" including speaker Ray Simpson from Lindisfarne, and the creation of a spiritual maze in the sand of St Brelade's Bay.

The same month saw St Brelade's on TV as the excavation of Neanderthal remains at La Cotte featured on BBC2's "Digging for Britain".

And two new heads took up their posts - John Baudains at Mont Nicolle, and Sarah Hague at Les Quennevais.

October and November you can read all about in this edition.

Christmas Edition 2013

Christmas Crackers Some of what we've groan to expect ....

Compiled by Tony Bellows

According to a magazine survey, here are the worst Christmas Cracker jokes:

What is Santa's favourite pizza?
One that's deep pan, crisp and even.

Why was Santa's little helper feeling depressed?
He had low elf-esteem.

What's furry and minty?
A polo bear.

How do snowmen get around?
They ride an icicle.

Who hides in the bakery at Christmas?
A mince spy.

What do you call a penguin in the Sahara desert?
Lost.

On which side do chickens have the most feathers?
The outside.

What's white and goes up?
A confused snowflake.

What do you call a woman who stands between two goal posts?
Annette.

What's green, covered in tinsel and goes ribbet ribbet?
Mistle-toad!

What do angry mice send each other at Christmas time?
Cross mouse cards

What bird is always out of breath?
A puffin

Christmas Edition 2013

Not a lot of people know that

From Church to Synagogue
by Michael Le Quesne

Where Petite Route des Mielles meets the main road is Tabor Synagogue. That was originally the site of a Wesleyan Methodist Chapel. Tabor Chapel was probably named after Mount Tabor, a location in in Galilee, believed to be the site of the transfiguration of Jesus. The Chapel was opened in 1825 and the original account books show pew rentals, in which wealthy families could rent pews for congregational worship, a practice which continued right up until 1962.

In 1905, members of the Tabor Chapel congregation had objected to playing golf on a Sunday. They could see the Headmaster of La Moye School, who was also the organist from another Church, frequently playing on the La Moye course as they passed close by. With the support of Captain Le Gallais, the Golf Club acquired land which allowed the holes to be moved to the west of the railway line, thus appeasing the church congregation.

Christmas Edition 2013

Parish Awash

Winter storms flood St. Aubin and cause damage

THE coincidence of high tides with a strong southerly winds and deep low pressure caused flooding and damage in late January and the road past the Parish Hall was awash with water, as waves crashed over the sea wall.

The spectacular picture above, taken by Jacqui Carrell, captures a wave as it breaks over the sea wall at St. Aubin between La Haule and Mont Les Vaux. Several properties were flooded and the road becoming impassable during the five high tides that co-incided with the late January storm.

La Baguette's reporter visited the shops along La Neuve Route to ask businesses how they coped with the flood waters.

At Chequers, the lady on the checkout said that they had kept the doors closed, with sandbags outside, which had kept the worst of the water at bay, with only a trickle seeping through. Citicab had also deployed sandbags, which had proven effective. Cheffins used sandbags, and while water did penetrate them, it came nowhere near the restaurant, which is well set back from the road.

Ashley Moore of "The Lab", however, decided to use a silicon sealant, as he felt that "sand being porous, would let water through eventually". He watched as the waters steadily climbed outside his shop front - "the road had become a fast flowing stream or small river". Fortunately, his sealant held, and his shop remained dry.

Restauranteur Murray Norton used rubber seals on the door of "Murrays" to good effect. He was also full of praise for the help given to businesses and home owners by the workers from TTS, engaged in the project to improve roads around the Parish Hall. "œThey were just fantastic, offering assistance and help with sandbags, and I couldn't praise them more," he said.

Constable Steve Pallett said "Our Honorary Police did a great job in redirecting traffic and in also deploying sandbags in various locations around St. Aubin to both protect businesses and of course the Parish Hall which, I am pleased to say, did not suffer any flooding."

The Met Office has reported a greater incidence of strong winds in January and February, and coupled with high tides, this will mean flooding could be more frequent, so that flood precautions at St Aubin may be needed more often.

Easter Edition 2014

Independent Thinking

Lost documents reveal Parish may not be part of Bailiwick
by Cristal Ireland & Connor Keefe

RECENTLY discovered ancient documents found last year in an old safe at the Parish Hall shed new light on Parish History.

At the same time in 1565 that Helier de Carteret, Seigneur of St. Ouen in Jersey, received Letters Patent from Queen Elizabeth I granting him Sark in fief in perpetuity, the Constable of St Brelade, Guillaume Bisson, received a Charter the Queen transferring the Vingtaines of Noirmont, Coin, Quennevais and La Moye to the Grand Duchy of Bouffon, "œesto perpetua, cum grano salis", as the Latin puts it.

As the Charter has never been revoked, St Brelade is legally part of Bouffon, and the States of Jersey have no legal jurisdiction over the Parish.

To this end, secret work behind the scenes has been taking place.

Last year, the harbour was dredged so that it would be sufficiently deep to receive vessels carrying freight, and this April, a new crane will be installed.

This will ensure St Brelade has an independent supply chain for essential commodities. Local accountants Murdstone and Grinby have also drawn up a budget to ensure that the Parish books are balanced.

A Parish Hall meeting was called for 1 April 2014, at which it was proposed that St Brelade becomes a GST exempt zone, and Parish revenues raised by the sale of duty free goods.

Various roads in and out of the Parish will have Toll gates erected at the Parish frontiers, so that other Islanders wishing to take advantage of the benefits of duty free shopping pay a modest fee to do so. This will go towards upkeep of the roads.

A special Bouffon Passport will also be issued for residents with the Parish Crest on its cover.

Negotiations have also taken place with the JEC to arrange an undersea cable to transfer power directly to the Parish, with the cable laid along the sea bed of St Aubin's Bay to La Collette.

It has also transpired from the Charter that any seafaring vessels passing within half a league of Corbiere, if berthing at St Aubin, must pay a levy.

On April 1, the Parish officially became the Independent Duchy of Bouffon, and a Vin d'Honneur was held at the newly opened Cafe Pesce d'Aprile on St Aubin's Bulwarks.

Easter Edition 2014

Podium Finish

'St. Brelades Bay Wave' makes for the shoreline!

THE St Brelade's Bay Hotel Podium Competition 2013 was won this year by Debbie Buterbaugh with a piece entitled "St Brelade's Bay Wave". This is a contemporary wave sculpture made from mild steel and recycled copper, with a centrepiece of driftwood and beach mosaic, to represent the beauty of the beach and the ocean.

Debbie explained how the bay inspired her. "When dreaming up a piece for the St Brelade's Bay Hotel, I pondered on what the Bay means to me and my family. St Brelade's Bay is our playground. When the kids were tiny we lived in Rectory Cottage and a walk along the Bay was part of the daily routine. Today we live up the hill and walk through Winston Churchill Park. We've spent many hours wandering the sand in search of treasure - delicate shells, pummelled beach glass, strange pebbles, and interesting pieces of pottery. The Bay is a paradise for locals and tourists alike. With all of this in mind I created St Brelade's Bay Wave."

She decided to use copper to represent the blues and greens of the sea, as copper develops a spectacular turquoise patina when left to the elements. This was achieved artificially by applying a liberal coating of salt and vinegar to the copper surface. The mosaic uses dark and light pebbles for contrast, and beach glass for added colour.

The artwork was officially unveiled on Friday 17 January 2014 Constable Steve Pallett, and will remain in place to view in the garden opposite the hotel for a year.

Home Comforts

Oakwell respite care home gets upgrade.

OAKWELL, the children's respite centre in St Brelade, is undergoing a £775,000 upgrade. The facility provides short breaks for children up to 18 with learning disabilities and/or physical disabilities. It is a 20 year old adapted 4-bedroom bungalow, but with additions of a Hydrotherapy Pool and sensory garden provided by the Variety Club.

Families whose lives involve round-the-clock care for their children really just need a break - a chance to do something that the rest of us often take for granted. But a recent Health and Social Services Scrutiny Panel review highlighted that the supply of residential respite care had experienced significant disruption in recent years. It reported that 'when a respite home is being used for emergency care, other families have not been able to access essential and short-term respite.' Following that review, a Ministerial decision was made by Deputy Anne Pryke to address the lack of adequate provision.

The new work will include increasing the number of bedrooms available from four to five, and a significant upgrade to amenities. All areas of the property will now be readily accessible for wheelchairs, and features will include a new sensory area, swimming pool, changing area and kitchen.

The funding for the project includes £50,000 from the Variety Club, and £25,000 from the Lions Club, who chose the project to be one of the prime beneficiaries of the 2014 Swimarathon.

Lions Club of Jersey President Chris Clarke said: "We are delighted to be able to make this commitment to Oakwell whilst also offering a further 25 Jersey children's charities the opportunity to benefit from the incredible fundraising of the Swimarathon participants."

Short breaks will be provided at Maison des Landes in St Ouen for the duration of the work, which should be completed by summer 2014

Easter Edition 2014

Appeal Ramps Up

St. Aubin on the Hill accessibility project on course

THE Church of St Aubin on the Hill has been busy fund raising and renovating to provide access to the main Church for wheelchair users, as well as a new toilet block at the rear, including a disabled toilet. Funds so far raised have reached £55,880.

The toilets are now complete, and were officially blessed on Sunday 9th March. Work is now proceeding with phase two. This will provide a ramp and railing with a new Northern entrance to the Porch with double doors. The old door will then be sealed, but has to remain in place to retain the "integrity" of the church. It is hoped that the work may be completed by Easter.

Fundraising committee member Denise Waller said that 'The good news is that we have raised all the money for the toilet block. The not-so-good news is that fund-raising must continue apace for the Disabled Access Phase 2 of this project. We are looking for a sponsor for the double doors which, with their ironmongery, and fitting will cost approximately £2,500.00. So any suggestions and offers will be gratefully received."

To contact Denise, tel 741941 email: waller@localdial.com

Easter Edition 2014

Living life to max

Former Deputy and Connétable, Max de la Haye shares memories

BORN in 1940, Max De La Haye has an early memory of being in the Royal Square with his father on Liberation Day in 1945, aged five.

His first school was Mrs O'Callaghan, who taught 20 children at her house by the top of Les Landes Avenue. There were a number of small establishments for young children from the ages of 5 to 7. He remembers getting a bicycle for Christmas and cycling it round her yard, with her chasing him, trying to catch him. "I was a mischievous child", he recalls.

From there it was to St Aubin's School (which is now St Aubin's College) for two years, for three years at Victoria College Prep, and Victoria College at 11 years old. He left early, in 1955, aged 15 - "I couldn't wait to get out of the place quickly, and back to the farm".

He remembers the teachers at school, often ex-army types, like Colonel Finch, whose bald head lit up like a red beacon when angry, and who was also a good shot with the blackboard duster. There were also "Dixie" Landick teaching German, "Paddy" Blomfield teaching woodwork, "Noddy" Salt teaching Latin, Reg Nicolle teaching P.E. His mischief didn't desert him, and he played a prank on one teacher using a potato to prevent the teacher's car from starting.

Leaving school, he worked on his father's farm, which was mixed, 12 milking cows, around 8 heifers, and growing potatoes, cauliflowers and tomatoes. It covered around 40 vergees, but when his father retired in 1970, Max rented more land, but gave up the livestock, concentrating on arable farming alone. There was also a good market for flowers for export.

As a young man, the place to go was West's in St Helier, where as well as cinema, there was ballroom dancing, and a chance to meet young ladies. Aged 17, he saw an advert for dancing lessons at West's - "in those days it was ballroom dancing - waltz, quickstep, and foxtrot".

It was there that he met Dot (Dorothy), and she was waiting for her bus on a Saturday night, when he passed her driving his father's Humber Hawk, and offered her a lift. They married in 1963, and went on 12 twelve day honeymoon in England, visiting Blackpool Tower, the Midlands, and Bournemouth. And they have been happily married ever since.

Easter Edition 2014

Fabric of the island

The Jersey Textile Showcase opened by Lt. Governor.

ON 5th March, the Lieutenant Governor, General Sir John McColl, officially opened the Jersey Textile Showcase at an Opening Party at the Harbour Gallery. Sir John thanked Pat Robson (both pictured opposite) and her team of volunteers for organising the events which he said were an amazing showcase of talent. Afterwards, a celebratory cake provided by Ann Pallett was enjoyed by all present.

The events ran until the 11 March, and included well attended workshops with UK and International textile tutors, covering such aspects as layering techniques, hot foiling, printing, spraying, and fabric decoration, embroidery, collages, wire and beads and also continental knitting techniques. One workshop even demonstrated the Bayeux stitch developed for the famous Bayeux Tapestry at the time when Jersey was still part of Normandy.

There were also free exhibitions of textile work submitted to the Open Competition at the Methodist Church on the Bulwarks, and St Aubin on the Hill Church. The latter also saw an exhibition of paintings and photography from Beaulieu Convent pupils, and small textile displays by children from Mont A L'Abbe school. Awards for all competitions were presented by Maggie Gray, editor of "Workshop on the Web" at a Gala Dinner held at the Somerville Hotel.

Easter Edition 2014

Not a lot know that

Grains of truth about place names
by Michael Le Quesne

St Brelade is a very sandy place, but not just down on its beaches. Place names give clues as to the sandy terrain inland.

Clos des Sables means the place of sand, and the word Mielle which lends itself to La Route des Mielles (the Five Mile Road) and La Petite Route des Mielles, means a sand-dune.

But the French word for "dune" is the same as the English.

The word "mielles" is actually Norman in origin, and may date as far back as 933 AD, when William Longsword made the Channel Islands part of Normandy.

Easter Edition 2014

Dirty Snowballs

Astronomy Club talk on comets

MARTIN Ahier gave an illustrated talk at the Jersey astronomy club on comets. Comets are icy bodies orbiting the solar system. An investigation of Halley's comet in 1986 supported astronomer Fred Whipple's idea that the nuclei of comets are essentially 'dirty snowballs'. The composition of a frozen water, carbon dioxide, methane and ammonia, in which dust and rocky material is embedded. The presence of nitrogen and carbon based compounds lends support to the theories that comets could have seeded the earth with life.

As a comet approaches the sun, solar heating starts to vapourize the ices, releasing gases that form a diffuse luminous sphere, called the "coma" around the nucleus. This is observable, but the nucleus itself is too small to be observed directly. Atoms swept away by the solar wind cause plasma and gas tails to emerge. The tails grow as they approach the sun and are always directed away from the sun; they can be as much as a hundred million kilometres long. As with sungrazer's like comet Ison last year, most do not survive an encounter with the sun, as gravitational forces tear it apart.

Easter Edition 2014

Carving out a hobby

Working with wood

IN 1987, Marvin Elliott came to Jersey to create a wooden sculpture "Resurrection" for St Ouen's Manor Chapel, starting an Evening Class in wood carving at Les Quennevais School.

Twenty-seven years later, now as a Club rather than an evening class, the Jersey Woodcarvers is still going strong, meeting at the school on Monday evenings from 7.30 to 9.30. They recently have had a welcome influx of young members, much to the delight of the Club leader, Eric Payn (pictured above).

The club has a small family atmosphere, and members have exhibited work at the Jersey Eisteddfod in the Art and Craft category. Last year, Arthur Morley, Eric Payn and Peter Wright all submitted pieces.

A wide variety of different styles and techniques are used by the club members, including pyrography, where wood is decorated with burn marks from the application of a heated object such as a wire-nib burners. Peter Wright uses this technique on some of his fine bird carvings to give texture.

Recently joined members told La Baguette that they enjoyed being part of a community rather than working alone, and appreciated the help given by the more experienced older hands, such as Eric Payn and Arthur Morley. "No skill is required to join" said Eric, "except patience!"

A modest fee of £35 pa includes Membership of the British Woodcarvers Association, and the insurance cover required by the Education Department.

For more information, contact Eric Payn on mobile 07797 729483 or by email at: eric.payn43@gmail.com.

Easter Edition 2014

Recipe Corner 1

Miriam's (Easter) Lemon Pudding

IN 1984 St Brelade's School on St Aubin's Hill closed because of falling numbers of pupils. The building is now a private language school, St Brelade's College. But when the school closed, a special commemorative book of cookery recipes was produced with submissions from former pupils and teachers.

This recipe was supplied by the Reverend Michael Halliwell (Rector of St Brelade) and his wife Sue. The school booklet notes that "œReverend was involved in some of our Advent and Christmas Services and in the Centenary in 1978.

Ingredients
Juice and rind of 1 lemon.
1 cup sugar
3 tablespoons flour
1 yolk egg
1cup milk
1 egg white well beaten

Preparation method
Mix sugar, lemon and flour and egg yolk till smooth. Add cup of milk slowly. Fold in beaten egg white. Pour into well greased dish. Stand dish in pan of hot water.
Bake in slow oven (275F / 140C / Gas Mark 1 for Â½ an hour. It should be firm on the top and runny underneath.

Easter Edition 2014

Recipe Corner 2

Pork Chops with Orange Sauce

ANOTHER recipe from the St. Brelade Cookbook. This warming recipe was given by the Dorothy Le Marquand, wife of the former President of Education, John Le Marquand whom he said was "the best cook I ever had".

John wrote about the school closure. "It. is all really a little sad. I have many memories of your school going back over many years. There were the Miss O'Neill's one of whom had been at the school for 63 years. She started at the age of 6 and worked there all her active and colourful life. I do not think that she was ever 'trained'. She was destined to teach and was much loved."

Ingredients: 4 Pork chops
3 ozs. Butter
Â½ lb. sliced onions
1 teaspoon mustard
1 teaspoon brown sugar
2 tablespoons plain flour
3 large oranges
Â½ pint stock or water
Â¼ pint. dry white wine
Salt. and black pepper

Method:

Remove excess fat from chops and mix together in bowl, mustard, sugar, black pepper, salt, and 2 ozs butter and spread on chops.
Fry sliced onions in 1 oz. butter and put in oven dish.
Fry chops 'till golden brown and put on top of the onions.
Mix flour, with. the butter left in the frying pan - add grated rind and juice of the oranges water or stock and wine - bring to the boil stirring well and pour over chops and onions.

Put dish in oven and cook slowly for about 1 hour at Gas 4 (350 F, 180C).

Easter Edition 2014